MASTERS AT WORK

BECOMING A NEUROSURGEON

BECOMING A VETERINARIAN

BECOMING A VENTURE CAPITALIST

BECOMING A HAIRSTYLIST

BECOMING A REAL ESTATE AGENT

BECOMING A MARINE BIOLOGIST

BECOMING AN ETHICAL HACKER

BECOMING A LIFE COACH

‹

BECOMING
A MARINE
BIOLOGIST

———————

VIRGINIA MORELL

SIMON & SCHUSTER

New York   London   Toronto   Sydney   New Delhi

Simon & Schuster
1230 Avenue of the Americas
New York, NY 10020

First Simon & Schuster hardcover edition April 2019

SIMON & SCHUSTER and colophon are registered trademarks
of Simon & Schuster, Inc.

For information about special discounts for bulk purchases,
please contact Simon & Schuster Special Sales at 1-866-506-1949
or business@simonandschuster.com.

The Simon & Schuster Speakers Bureau can bring authors to your
live event. For more information or to book an event, contact the
Simon & Schuster Speakers Bureau at 1-866-248-3049
or visit our website at www.simonspeakers.com.

Manufactured in the United States of America

1   3   5   7   9   10   8   6   4   2

Library of Congress Cataloging-in-Publication Data is available.

ISBN 978-1-5011-8120-7
ISBN 978-1-5011-8121-4 (ebook)

In memory of my parents,
who shared with me their love of
the natural world, its special places,
and all its creatures.

CONTENTS

Chapter One   1

Chapter Two   15

Chapter Three   31

Chapter Four   53

Chapter Five   71

Chapter Six   91

Chapter Seven   109

Chapter Eight   123

Chapter Nine   149

Epilogue   171
Sources   181
Further Reading   187

BECOMING
A MARINE
BIOLOGIST

1

"Fin!" shouted Colin Cornforth. "There's a fin up!" He squinted at the horizon. "Three animals. Make that four at eleven o'clock. Risso's, maybe." Chopping the air with the side of his hand, Cornforth, a captain with a tour company in Kona, Hawai'i, pointed in the direction the dolphins were traveling.

Dr. Robin Baird nodded and steered the twenty-four-foot Zodiac toward the animals but didn't increase his speed. Baird has been studying the behaviors of the whales and dolphins of the Hawaiian Islands for almost twenty years. He knew that the sound of a boat's motor frightens some sea mammals, and did not want to spook them. Risso's dolphins are a rarely seen species he's targeted on this two-week survey off the Big Island of Hawai'i—part of his long-term study of the cetaceans (the general term for whales and dolphins) that live or spend time in the islands' waters.

"I've got seven animals now!" Cornforth called out from the prow.

Baird nodded again and smiled. Only fifteen minutes prior, Cornforth and the three other crew members had been muttering, bored by Baird's choice of routes for the day. The team had left the Kona dock at 5:25 a.m., and headed north to these waters. We were six miles offshore, where the sea extends nearly a mile and a half below the surface. It's the region Baird most loves to explore. "This is where the pelagic species live," he explained, using the term for deepwater sea creatures, such as "false killer whales, beaked and Bryde's whales, rough-toothed and Risso's dolphins. These are animals that people don't often see."

There was no guarantee, of course, that we would see them, either. Dolphins don't leave tracks or scents as land mammals do. The only way to find them is by motoring around and sighting a fin in the distance, or a splash and some spray. You might get lucky—or you might not. And we'd been unlucky for almost six hours. Moments before spotting the Risso's dolphins, Cornforth had groused—just loud enough for me to hear—that the day was being wasted "traveling across this desert."

Baird, a tall and beefy ginger-haired man with eyes as blue as the sea, stood beneath the shady shelter of his inflatable boat's canvas awning. For someone with such fair skin, Hawai'i's sun and the glare from the water posed a danger, and he dressed accordingly: long-sleeved shirt, long pants, and visor—and now and then rubbed more sunscreen over his nose and cheeks. He didn't react to Cornforth's jibe. After all, he'd used the word *desert* himself when describing the region to me the day before. The Hawaiian Islands, Baird explained, create oases in the midst of the Pacific Ocean's desert—so named because it's largely poor in nutrients. The trade winds and ocean currents stir only the surface waters, except around the islands; their size and height break up the winds and currents so that the cold, nutrient-rich waters of the deep mix with the warm, oxygen-poor surface waters, causing the water to bloom with phytoplankton, the microscopic algae that are the basis of the ocean's food webs. Where phytoplankton are abundant, so are squid and fish, and their predators, including dolphins and whales.

Twenty-five species of cetaceans live near the Hawaiian Islands. Eighteen are odontocetes: toothed animals such as common bottlenose and Risso's dolphins, and killer and sperm whales. The other seven are baleen whales (also known as mysticetes), such as humpback, fin, and blue whales, which have plates of baleen (made of the protein keratin) that sieve the water as they feed on plankton and krill. Most tourists—

and most scientists—typically see only two of these twenty-five species: humpback whales and spinner dolphins, which are easy to spot from shore or on whale-watching cruises. Baird has made the other twenty-three species his specialty.

"Hawai'i was a very crowded place for whale researchers when I first came here in 1998," he told me. But it was only crowded if you were studying the obvious suspects. Indeed, as Baird began to search for his niche, he made a discovery: in the preceding thirty years, nearly every research article about Hawai'i's cetaceans focused on either humpbacks or spinner dolphins. At the time, this sort of concentration on one or two species wasn't unusual in cetacean research. For example, most researchers in British Columbia, Canada, focused only on killer whales, while a few also studied gray whales. That left plenty of room for an observant and determined young scientist to build his own research project, Baird realized. And so he did.

Of course, doing so wasn't easy or straightforward. He was poor most of the time and stressed by the need to secure grants, get boats and crews, digest the data they collected, and write papers—often simultaneously. But over time, he made discoveries and published enough papers that other cetacean experts tipped their hats to his accomplishments.

"I never would have thought you could do what Baird's

done—see these rare cetaceans regularly enough to gather the kind of data he has," said Scott Baker, a conservation geneticist and cetacean specialist at the Oregon State University Marine Mammal Institute. Like many of the young marine biologists at the University of Hawai'i in the 1980s, Baker had researched humpback whales for his dissertation. "But Robin saw the potential in these offshore, more unpredictable species." His work has "helped fill in some big gaps." The two men met in the early 1980s at a conference and now collaborate on a number of projects to study and conserve cetaceans.

Baird has never given his project an official title. He refers to it simply as "our Hawai'i research" or "Hawai'i cetaceans." Officially, he's a research biologist with Cascadia Research Collective in Olympia, Washington, a nonprofit research and education organization that he joined in 2003. Through the collective, he applies for grants and contracts primarily from US government agencies such as the National Marine Fisheries Service (NMFS), the Pacific Islands Fisheries Science Center (PIFSC), the Marine Mammal Commission (MMC), and the US Navy. One approximately $100,000 grant to study the islands' populations of false killer whales—five to six foot long cousins of killer whales; they have a pale blaze between their pectoral fins and a light stripe down the belly but otherwise are almost solidly dark gray—came from

NMFS's Bycatch Reduction Engineering Program, an effort to lower the number of these whales caught accidentally by fishers. The funds covered the costs of the survey I joined, as well as the subsequent data analysis and report preparation, and contributed to Baird's and his team members' salaries.

TEN MINUTES AFTER CORNFORTH first spotted the Risso's dolphins, Baird managed to work his boat just behind them. About two dozen swam ahead of us, rising quickly and rhythmically to expel the air in their lungs before inhaling and diving back into the water. The air filled with the *whoosh* of their wet breaths. In the distance, they appeared silvery white, with dark, rounded heads and hooked dorsal fins. Closer up, we could see that they're actually gray-black in hue, the front half of their bodies crisscrossed with intricate white scars resembling scribbled gang graffiti. Newborn Risso's have black backs and sides, Baird explained, but the animals become lighter as they age and accumulate scars from playing and fighting—and from being attacked by both their prey (squid) and their predators (sharks).

"This is only our eleventh encounter in eighteen years with this species," Baird said, "and we've only put a satellite tag on one, so we don't know a lot about their behaviors." He

Risso's Dolphin

stood behind the steering wheel, slowly and steadily scanning the waters, keeping an eye on the Risso's while checking the horizon for other dolphins or whales.

"Risso's avoid boats here in Hawai'i, although not in Southern California," he continued. "Here they're part of an open ocean population and not accustomed to motors, so we're just going to hang with them." He cut the boat's motor, and the dolphins slowed their pace. A dozen lined up close together in what Baird called a raft formation, with their pectoral fins touching—a dolphin's version of holding hands—and rode the waves next to the Zodiac. This is a form of "slow travel," Baird said, which allows the dolphins to rest. They'd likely been awake most of the night, hunting squid.

This group was apparently untroubled by our presence, and while some stayed together in their quiet raft, others began leaping over the waves and chasing one another. It looked like fun, and Baird said it probably was. "That's social behavior," he explained. "They're playing, and maybe courting." He called to Cornforth and a deeply tanned young woman standing next to him on a platform above the prow. Both had cameras pressed to their faces. "Let's be sure we get ID photos of them all!" Baird was just starting to build an ID catalog of this species.

"We're getting them," said the woman, Kimberly Wood, a marine mammal photographer and research associate on Baird's project. She and Cornforth use Canon cameras with 400-millimeter lenses to collect images of the dolphins' fins and scarred backs as the animals come to the surface. Each dolphin had its own unique scarring pattern, which the scientists would later use to identify individuals—hoping to match the day's photos with others they'd shot previously. Over time the scientists would be able to see which dolphins like spending time together—simple clues that could provide deeper insights into their social organization and family ties.

"Birds at one o'clock!" called out Cornforth, the crew's top spotter. Baird turned his binoculars on the birds skimming the water. "Shearwaters," he said, identifying the species for Brittany Guenther, at twenty-six, the youngest member of the team, and a volunteer. Guenther had earned a bachelor of science in marine biology at the College of Charleston and loves the sea, but she disliked school; the South Carolina native is now working on becoming a boat captain in Maui, the second largest Hawaiian island. Her main job on Baird's crew—aside from watching for whales and dolphins—was keeping a data sheet of the mammals, fish, and birds we saw and their behaviors.

Guenther had met Baird in 2017 at a Whale Tales Conference, an annual four-day event in Maui that brings together marine experts from around the world. After attending his lecture about his book *The Lives of Hawai'i's Dolphins and Whales: Natural History and Conservation*, which distills his research through 2016, she asked him to sign her copy—and took the opportunity to offer to help on his upcoming project on the small island of Lana'i. Baird agreed, and she was part of the team for four days. "Generally, when folks who work on the water in Hawai'i express an interest, I invite them out for a day," he said. "I didn't know if she would work out but am always willing to let someone come out once."

Guenther, who readily pitched in on all tasks and was eager to learn, had clearly worked out.

Baird works on projects off all the main Hawaiian Islands and makes a point of contacting whale-watching companies, fishermen, captains, and interested citizen-scientists to let them know what he is doing and why. He asks them to report any cetacean sightings and send him photos of the animals they encounter; if he uses their images in his publications, he gives them credit. His outreach has paid off with an abundance of sightings and photos he would have missed otherwise. Regular contributors are often invited to join as a volunteer for a day. Indeed, nearly every day on the two-week survey I joined, Baird included one amateur whale-watcher: marine biologists, teachers, or hopeful photographers. If they prove to be good workers, like Guenther, they are often invited back as volunteers on a longer survey.

Baird's last permanent team member, Daniel Webster, stayed near the prow, holding an air rifle and watching for an adult dolphin to surface alongside the Zodiac. If that happened, he would fire a titanium dart with a satellite tag at the dolphin's dorsal fin. The tags, which don't harm the animals, can remain attached for weeks or even months, collecting data on the dolphin's movements and diving behaviors. (The scientists obtain the data via orbiting weather satellites.) Webster first successfully attached a tag to a Risso's dolphin in 2015. According to Baird, "That dolphin kept to the deep waters to the west of Kona and the island of Lana'i. Based on his movements, and our other encounters, we think that Risso's aren't resident dolphins here in Hawai'i"—a finding that will help determine how federal agencies manage the species. Resident species, as opposed to animals passing through, are more likely to be affected by local activities, such as near-shore fisheries and US Navy sonar training activities.

We traveled with the Risso's for about an hour. Webster never did get his shot, and when the raft of dolphins split apart and the animals picked up speed, Baird turned his boat away, thinking it best to let them travel on their own.

"Reason for leaving?" Guenther asked.

"All ID'd," Baird said.

Guenther marked her data sheet while Baird leaned back on his captain's seat and slowly scanned the seas, on the hunt again for dolphins and whales.

PRIOR TO BAIRD'S RESEARCH, scientists thought that most toothed-whale species were, like these Risso's dolphins, simply visitors to the Hawaiian Islands, and so their distribution (that is, which areas they preferred), movements, and numbers were not tracked. Because of Baird, scientists now know that eleven species of odontocetes actually live around the islands all year. His studies have led NMFS to recognize that several species, including pantropical spotted dolphins, false killer whales, bottlenose dolphins, and melon-headed whales, have populations associated with specific islands—a finding that influences such things as seismic surveys and naval exercises. Scott Baker praises Baird's work, calling it "a breakthrough discovery," that "really changed how we think about these animals and how they use the islands. Clearly, the islands are more than just oases for some cetaceans. They are their home."

Four times every year, for two weeks at a time, Baird and his crew travel around the Hawaiian islands, watching for fins and splashes. They observe and photograph the species they encounter, and, when they can, attach satellite tags to some animals, and collect a small amount of tissue for later genetic analysis and other research. When he's not on the water, Baird's reviewing the photographs and data his team has collected, tracking the tagged cetaceans (he can view them on his office computer in Washington State), and writing up research papers; he's authored or coauthored hundreds of these, as well as conference presentations, *The Lives of Hawai'i's Dolphins and Whales*, and another popular and acclaimed book, *Killer Whales of the World: Natural History and Conservation*.

Baird is modest about his accomplishments and always generously gives credit to his team and research colleagues. But he also, somewhat shyly, marvels at how his childhood love of animals led him to become what he so clearly is: the world's leading expert on the dolphins and whales of Hawai'i.

2

"Oh, I remember exactly when I met Robin Baird," said Dave Duffus, a marine biologist at the University of Victoria on Vancouver Island, Canada. "He just came to my office one day in 1985. He was a third-year undergraduate and said, 'I hear you're going to do some fieldwork on killer whales. If you are, I'm your guy.'"

Baird's direct manner surprised Duffus, who was a well-known ecologist and associate professor in the university's Geography Department, and used to somewhat shyer, more timid students. He had just applied for a research grant to study the effects of whale watching on the orcas (as killer whales are also called) in Johnstone Strait, off the Vancouver Island coast. If the grant were approved, Duffus would want a field assistant—and indeed, someone just like Baird. "He's a big guy, and was young and strong. He looked like he could take care of himself," Duffus recalled, "so I told him I'd let him know."

To ensure that the professor remembered him, Baird became a regular visitor to his office, although he never took any of his courses. "He basically camped out here," Duffus said. "We'd sit around and chat." Baird wasn't particularly forthcoming about his personal life ("a closed book," Duffus called him), but he opened up when the subject turned to killer whales. "He was really knowledgeable," Duffus continued. "He'd read the scientific literature and could cite all the key studies. And he was incredibly driven. He was already photographing orcas from a small patched-up boat he had."

Baird was then twenty-two and, despite Duffus's assessment, not yet dead set on studying killer whales. "I wanted to be a wildlife biologist," Baird recalled, sitting on the deck of the home he'd rented for his crew in Kona. He'd poured himself a glass of wine and me one of lemonade, and relaxed at a table overlooking the home's lush gardens while keeping his binoculars close at hand in case he spotted a rare species of bird. His wife, fellow marine biologist Annie Douglas, and one-year-old son, Bryson, were resting in the nearby guesthouse. "I was just interested in animals," Baird continued. "Whatever species I was studying at any given moment was the one I wanted to spend the rest of my life studying. For a while, it was invertebrates (animals without backbones), then reptiles and amphibians, then birds, and finally whales."

Somewhat counterintuitively, Baird's catholic interests helped him become an excellent marine biologist. Bird watching in particular taught him to pay attention to detail, a key skill for cetacean researchers.

Growing up on Vancouver Island, Baird had plenty of opportunities to see whales and other marine mammals. But he rarely did, although he and an older brother spent time at the seashore collecting animals they saw in tide pools. He also read voraciously, especially the British naturalist Gerald Durrell's books about his childhood adventures on the island of Corfu, and his exotic collecting trips to Africa. By the time he was eleven, Baird knew his life's calling: he would work with animals, most probably in a zoo.

By then, Baird had seen killer whales, his first encounter coming at a public aquarium, Sealand of the Pacific, where his mother took him to see two captured orcas: Haida and a partial albino named Chimo. A few years later, he finally saw orcas in the wild: a group of about fifty, swimming close to shore. He and his parents watched from the Victoria waterfront as they dived and surfaced. He had no inkling that he would spend many years of his life chasing after *these* creatures—he was too enthralled by animals in general—but the power, beauty, and mystery of the whales still left "an indelible imprint."

The youngest of five children, Baird vaguely understood that he would need a college degree to study animals, or even to work in a zoo. But formal education wasn't valued highly at home. Neither of his parents graduated college, although his father worked in the computer department of the provincial government, and several of Baird's siblings had gone to work and never completed high school. While his parents loved reading—stacks of books filled the shelves of their home from ceiling to floor—their expectations for their children "were probably very low," he reflected. "Several of my siblings had seriously misbehaved, and they figured I would, too."

Baird's love of reading helped him secure top grades in elementary and middle school but marked him as an introvert. He'd also act out occasionally, pulling pranks such as starting a fire near an apartment complex and taking bullets he'd found in his parents' garage to a construction site and then dropping large rocks onto them. Then there was the time he got picked up for shoplifting. "My dad did whack me a couple of times for things like that, but I deserved it," Baird said with a shrug.

In high school he had only a few friends—until the day an older brother handed him a small bag of marijuana to sell. "I went from being unpopular to being very popular in a short period of time," he said, chuckling. But his grades suffered, and he became a problem student. One day Baird lit a "small fire" in his school desk and was suspended for a time. "It wasn't really me," he says now of his teenage behavior, "just my response to peer pressure and my older brother." He was saved by dating a straightlaced girl "who didn't drink or smoke." In her company, Baird found he "was no longer motivated to do those things." So he quit. At last, unlike some of his older siblings, Baird graduated from high school—although he didn't see it as much of an accomplishment at the time. "My parents were overjoyed," he said, "but I really didn't know what I would do after high school."

Baird had long since abandoned his dreams of becoming a biologist. He'd never been particularly good at math and so had dropped the subject after tenth grade. For the same reason, he'd skipped physics and chemistry. "I was afraid of those classes," he said. Still, he enrolled in two courses—Introductory Psychology and Basic Philosophy—at the local two-year school, Camosun College. The philosophy course got him interested in learning again, and the psychology class revealed another path to studying animals. "Many animal behavior studies at that time were done in psychology departments," Baird recalled. "So I planned to major in psychology and minor in biology"—a route that would let him avoid math, physics, and chemistry.

At Camosun, the small class size and the enthusiastic faculty rekindled Baird's love for biology. The first course he took was on invertebrates and to learn more about them, Baird started scuba diving. He learned to drive a boat, too, and the more time he spent on the water, the more he began to think about becoming a marine biologist. Baird decided to major in biology after all, even joining the nonprofit research group the International Cetacean Watch Society, with one instructor's encouragement. That summer, he forced himself to take math, physics, and chemistry—and passed all three.

From community college, Baird transferred to the University of Victoria, where he enrolled in a class on the biology of vertebrates and soon became enamored of birds. He spent his free time wandering the forests and shore, learning to identify all the local species and honing his observational skills—to be quiet and patient and attentive to small details. The noted research university also offered young biologists a chance to gain work experience between semesters. He attended four months of school, and then worked at a job for the next four months, which counted toward his degree. Baird's first position took him back to the sea, measuring edible mollusks called abalones for a private company. He then moved on to the British Columbia Department of Wildlife, working in a program to reintroduce burrowing owls to the wild. His third job would be the one he'd pestered Professor Dave Duffus about: working as a research assistant studying killer whales. And his fourth job, which he took on in the fall of 1986, right after assisting Duffus, saw him working for Canada's Department of Fisheries and Oceans (DFO), determining the sex of prawns. Each position paid a small wage.

Around 1987, Baird's girlfriend, Pam Stacey, began working at the DFO's office in the city of Nanaimo on the east coast of Vancouver Island. There she met Michael Bigg, a fiftyish marine biologist and legendary pioneer of killer whale research. She volunteered on Bigg's project, and introduced Baird to him. The meeting came at a propitious time for a young biologist at the start of his career. In the mid-1980s, scientists were only just beginning to study killer whales. Indeed, so little was known about the animals that just two decades earlier, killer whales had been considered fierce predators, with governments throughout the world encouraging fishermen to shoot and kill them. From 1962 to 1973, aquariums captured for public display forty-seven orcas from the waters around British Columbia and Washington State, including Chimo and Haida, whom Baird remembered so fondly from childhood. At least twelve orcas died during these attempts. Since no one had conducted a proper survey of the region's killer whale population—or any orca population—wildlife officials couldn't say if such captures were sustainable. Finally, in 1970 the Canadian government hired Michael Bigg to find out.

The marine biologist sent fifteen thousand questionnaires to fishermen, lighthouse keepers, and boaters, asking them to record any killer whale sightings they made on one day: July 27, 1971. The results shocked everyone: a mere 350 orcas inhabited the waters of western British Columbia. Subsequent surveys confirmed the count. The practice of capturing the mammals was banned.

While working on his survey, Bigg began photographing the markings of every killer whale he saw and soon realized that each animal's black-and-white pattern was distinctive— a finding that revolutionized the field. As he reported in 1973, each orca had its own uniquely shaped and nicked dorsal fin, as well as its own light-gray saddle patch behind that fin, a unique white eyespot, and personal body scars. By photographing every killer whale they encountered, Bigg and his colleagues could identify each one and thus survey an entire population without interfering in the orcas' lives. Photo identification became the standard field tool for whale researchers around the world.

While Pam Stacey was working for Bigg, she met research-

Killer Whale

ers from around the world who sought the pioneering killer whale researcher's advice. That was what brought Thomas Lyrholm, a Swedish marine biologist, to Vancouver Island that summer. Keen to study killer whales in Iceland, Lyrholm lacked field experience, so Bigg suggested he start by observing the killer whales around Race Rocks at the southern tip of Vancouver Island. Stacey and Baird offered to accompany him, Robin to drive the boat and Pam to take photos.

The trio devised a simple spotting technique. Each day,

they climbed the Race Rocks Lighthouse and watched for killer whales. As soon as they saw a pod, they ran down the stairs, hopped in their boat, and followed the whales. "It all seemed incredibly easy," Baird told me, smiling at the memory and his naïve perception of what whale research entailed.

Their gear was simple, too. The boat was a twelve-foot aluminum cartopper—one that was easily placed atop their car. Someone gave them life jackets, and he and Stacey sold their scuba diving equipment and bought cameras. Bigg provided the film. And yet despite the inexpensive and low-tech nature of the project, and almost unintentionally, Baird was gaining field expertise—something of key importance to anyone contemplating a career in wildlife biology.

Baird loved the fieldwork and realized, too, that he loved reading research papers and the detailed knowledge they imparted. Before Duffus's project, Baird eagerly attended the 1985 International Marine Mammal Conference in Vancouver, where he was, he admitted, "overwhelmed"—but in a way he found exciting. "There were so many papers, so many sessions, so many people to meet," he remembered. "And so much to learn." By the conference's end, he was ready to commit to becoming a marine biologist—and, more specifically, a cetacean expert.

Baird would need to attend graduate school for a PhD, but

his grades were not the best. In classes he didn't like, Baird eked out Cs; however, in those he enjoyed, he pulled down As and Bs. "He was just not a great student," Duffus said. The young man wasn't a slacker—but he was used to being independent and self-sufficient; more of "a field naturalist" than an academic. Duffus suggested Baird might need to find an alternate path.

But Baird didn't want to reconsider his career. Not just because of his passion for studying whales—because of the people. The young man seldom discussed his private life, but his parents had recently died within a couple of years of each other, from lung cancer. He missed them "every day." Baird fell out of touch with his immediate older brother, who had bullied him, and seldom saw his other siblings. The cetacean community provided what he'd lost: support from others, and the sense that his life had meaning and purpose.

After graduating from the University of Victoria in 1987, Baird put off deciding whether to apply for graduate school; instead, he and Stacey spent the year photographing whales for Bigg. They had access to a better boat, one that a local businessman bought for whale-watching tours. Pam worked as the naturalist on these outings while Robin drove; he was living on unemployment insurance from the jobs he'd worked during college. When there were no passengers, the owner let them take out the boat for free to look for whales. On one such outing, he and Stacey saw something unexpected: a pod of killer whales hunting and eating harbor seals. They told Bigg, who said that he, too, had witnessed this behavior, but only a few times. "If you see it again," he told them, "be sure you record it, because it is rare." Over the next few months, they documented eight additional incidents.

The amateurs' sightings helped confirm Bigg's hypothesis that two types of killer whales, as he always called orcas, occupied the same Pacific Northwest waters. One fed solely on fish; he called these the "resident killer whales," because they stayed in the area year-round. The other type traveled through the coastal waters, staying awhile before moving on, and dined primarily on marine mammals; Bigg called these the "transient killer whales." Baird loved to write almost as much as he loved reading—a boon for a scientist's career—and now he had data for his first peer-reviewed research papers, which he coauthored with Stacey. Their first, published in the major scientific publication the *Canadian Journal of Zoology*, made public their discovery that the two types of killer whales had noticeably different saddle patches. The finding suggested the populations were reproductively isolated, and thus, as Michael Bigg hypothesized, likely separate species.

Baird and Stacey's second paper discussed their observation that harbor seals usually recognized and fled from the dangerous orcas but were unperturbed by those that had bent dorsal fins. Apparently, the seals did not recognize such animals as killer whales. They published this in the *Canadian Field-Naturalist*, another peer-reviewed journal. Having their work accepted by these highly regarded academic publications was a significant accomplishment for two young people who'd only just graduated with bachelor of science degrees.

GRADUATE SCHOOL APPLICATION SEASON came and went, and still Baird didn't apply. "I was just not interested," he confessed. "I couldn't imagine getting to work on what I wanted to do [study wild killer whales], and the thought of doing graduate work on something else" held no appeal. He'd taken only one basic statistics course, and so fell short of the requirements for most marine biology programs. Then one day in the fall of 1987, Robin noticed a flyer posted on a bulletin board at the Whale Museum in Friday Harbor, San Juan Island, announcing the formation of a research group focused on behavioral ecology—very similar to what he'd been studying with killer whales. The program was at Simon Fraser University, on the mainland. A few months later, he traveled to Vancouver and dropped in unannounced on the program's director, Dr. Larry Dill.

"He came to my office and said, 'I want to study whales,'" Dill recalled. "Well, okay. I get about twenty of these wide-eyed whale huggers every year, and I just figured he was another one. But then he said, 'I've been studying killer whales, and I have some data you might want to look at.'"

Baird's words startled Dill, who had by chance just finished reading a new book coauthored by Bigg: *Killer Whales: A Study of Their Identification, Genealogy & Natural History in British Columbia and Washington State*. Dill was neither a marine biologist nor a field scientist. He was an ecologist. His students worked with fish, insects, and birds—animals they could care for in a lab and use as tools to answer questions about predator-prey relationships and foraging behaviors. How, for instance, do animals decide where to search for food, and how does the presence of predators affect those decisions? Reading Bigg's book had left him curious about killer whales; since individual orcas could be identified in the wild, Dill thought they might be good subjects for studying the issues that interested him. "I'd actually been thinking that I'd like to get a graduate student started on this," he recalled. "And here was Robin, who was already working with the whales and had data he'd already collected. He was a very good writer, too."

Dill didn't want a student to simply follow killer whales and describe their activities. He wanted someone who thought like a scientist and could come up with questions to test: How did transient killer whales choose where to hunt their prey? Which pods had the most reproductive success? How did the number and sex of individual orcas in a pod affect its hunting success? Did their foraging behaviors influence their social organization and reproductive success? Did social behaviors differ between resident and transient killer whales?

Listening to Dill, Baird realized this was what he'd been searching for: a mentor who could help him become a scientist; someone who would take his love of the natural world and show him how to shape it into scientific inquiry, to ask important questions. For his part, Dill could not believe his good fortune.

Baird started working on a master of science degree with Dill in September 1988.

3

If you're looking to become a marine biologist, be forewarned: a broad range of positions fall within that title. Most marine biologists study the organisms that live in the sea: organisms that vary greatly, from microscopic viruses, plankton, and bacteria, to Earth's largest creatures, the blue whales. Planktologists, ichthyologists (fish scientists), fishery biologists, microbiologists, ecologists, and marine mammalogists can all be marine biologists—as can hydrologists and physical oceanographers, who study the sea's physical properties and how these affect marine life. Marine biologists more interested in managing marine resources may also become economists, sociologists, environmental managers, chemists, and pollution experts.

It's somehow fitting that marine biology—basically, the study of life in the sea—is such a vast field, since the ocean covers 71 percent of Earth's surface, making it the largest habitat on our planet—and one of its most varied. Yet this habitat is also among the least studied. Only a small portion of the seafloor, between 5 percent and 15 percent, has been mapped. From that alone, we know that the underwater landscape includes towering mountain ranges, trenches deeper than the Grand Canyon, muscular rock formations, exploding volcanoes, kelp forests, and seagrass meadows. It's the job of marine biologists to understand how the organisms that swim or drift through these little-known lands have evolved and adapted to life in the deep, often in complete darkness; how they interact with their habitat and one another; and how we can protect them from human activities.

The study of marine life is thought to date back to at least the ancient Phoenicians, who undertook a series of ocean voyages in 1200 BC using their knowledge of tides, currents, landmarks, and seasons, as well as celestial navigation, while relying on the ocean's bounty. They often sailed to trade with the Land of Punt (thought to be modern Somalia), and south along the East African coast, as well as throughout the Mediterranean. But the Greek philosopher-naturalist Aristotle was the first to record his observations of marine life, making him the undisputed father of marine biology. In around 300 BC, he identified crustaceans, echinoderms (sea stars, sea urchins, sand dollars), mollusks, and fish, and recognized that cetaceans are mammals. (People sometimes mistake whales and dolphins for fish, but they give birth to live young and nurse their calves from their mammary glands.)

Most ancient peoples relied on the sea for food but did not develop a systematic way of cataloging or understanding the animals they caught. So while the Polynesians were great navigators, fishers, and explorers—sailing and settling lands from New Zealand, to Easter Island, to Hawai'i—they did not contribute to the development of marine biology as a field of science.

The field—and the biological sciences in general—blossomed during the European Age of Discovery, beginning in the fifteenth century, when explorers such as Christopher Columbus and Vasco da Gama made their great maritime journeys, crossing the Atlantic to the Americas, and sailing around Africa's Cape of Good Hope to India, respectively. They returned with plants and animals previously unknown in Europe, which inspired a growing interest in natural history.

When Captain James Cook sailed the *Endeavour* to Oceania from 1768 to 1771, two naturalists trained in the Linnaean taxonomic system were invited along: the men recorded thousands of species of plants and animals then unknown in Britain and Europe, such as breadfruit, various orchids, golden-crested penguins, and kangaroos.

The British sea captain circumnavigated the world twice during his lifetime. Cook's voyages of exploration are considered the beginning of the modern study of marine biology. His discoveries inspired English schoolboys, including Charles Darwin, to study marine life. As the resident naturalist aboard the HMS *Beagle*, Darwin made good use of Cook's three-volume *A Voyage to the Pacific Ocean* during his five-year journey (1831 to 1836) around the world, with extensive stops in coastal South America and the Galápagos Islands. On this voyage, Darwin studied the formation of coral reefs and collected marine organisms for the British Museum, including one particularly fascinating miniscule, shell-less barnacle that he found on an archipelago near Chile. Darwin discovered the barnacle after picking up a conch shell that was riddled with holes. On board the *Beagle*, Darwin placed the shell under his microscope—and spotted inside one of the cavities a tiny barnacle that was invisible to the naked eye. He knew the barnacle was new to science and puzzled over its lack of a shell. This was an important, diagnostic feature—one that most taxonomists at that time would have seized on as an example of a deviation from an "ideal" type. But Darwin realized that being shell-less was actually a response or adaptation to living life in a different manner than did barnacles that had shells.

When he returned to England, Darwin spent eight years cataloging his barnacle collection, as well as fossil barnacles and hundreds of other barnacles scientists from around the world sent him by mail. Many barnacles, he found, had been misclassified; overall, they varied greatly in their morphology and reproductive adaptations, and had clearly changed through time. Darwin published four serious monographs on barnacles, making him the world's authority and establishing his reputation as a major figure in British zoology. His study of a single entire group of organisms, living and fossilized, also helped him understand how such diversity might have developed over time. Historians of science credit Darwin's barnacle research as being as important to the development of his theory of evolution as his study of the Galápagos Island finches.

Britain continued to lead the young field of marine biology, with the Royal Society sponsoring another scientific voyage in 1872. Just before Christmas that year, the HMS *Challenger*, a refurbished warship outfitted with laboratories and scientific equipment, set sail from Portsmouth on a four-year journey. The crew circumnavigated and crisscrossed the world, from the Strait of Gibraltar and the Canary Islands to Bermuda and Nova Scotia, before sailing south to Brazil, and east to the Cape of Good Hope—a tour of some seventy thousand nautical miles. The *Challenger* sailed close to Antarctica, and visited Australia, New Zealand, many Pacific islands, Patagonia, the Strait of Magellan, and the Falkland Islands, before finally returning to port in Hampshire, England, in 1876. She was loaded with the best science and technology equipment of the day, including specimen jars, microscopes, trawls, dredges, thermometers and barometers, and devices to collect sediment from the seabed. Sir Charles Wyville Thomson, a noted and influential naturalist at the University of Edinburgh, had proposed the expedition and helped Captain George Nares select the crew and scientists, which included two additional naturalists and two oceanographers, as well as an artist to draw the specimens. Captain Nares also employed expert navigators who collaborated with the others to map the sea and explore the ocean floor.

Equipped with 181 miles of rope and lead weights, the *Challenger*'s crew made almost five hundred soundings of the sea bottom and discovered the deepest part of the ocean: the Mariana Trench in the western Pacific, where the seafloor is more than 36,074 feet (or more than seven miles) deep. The scientists also discovered undersea mountains such as the mid-Atlantic Ridge, charted the oceans' currents, and gathered thousands of specimens—many of them new species, including 4,700 marine organisms. Perhaps most significantly for marine biologists, the *Challenger*'s research team disproved the previously accepted hypothesis of the British naturalist Edward Forbes that nothing could live below 1,800 feet in the sea.

Disproving this false idea changed how scientists regarded the sea, since they now realized there must be thousands, perhaps millions, of unknown species inhabiting what they had discovered to be a surprisingly diverse terrain. As the first true oceanographic cruise, the *Challenger* accomplished what its organizers envisioned: it laid the groundwork for oceanography as a field of study.

Scientists on these early expeditions were hampered by the equipment they used—nets, buckets, and dredges—to bring up creatures from the deep, which were often crushed during the ascent. The only sea life they could observe in a natural habitat was that of the intertidal zone: the part of the shore that is above the water at low tide and underwater when the tide is high. What they collected, though, fascinated them—and hinted that the living world of the watery depths was as rich and diverse as that on land. (Indeed, some researchers were correct in suspecting that underwater life was more so.) To better understand the hidden layers of the ocean, Germany built a marine biological station—the first of its kind—in Naples, Italy, in 1872; an American station soon followed at Penikese Island, Massachusetts. (This facility would evolve into the prestigious Marine Biological Laboratory at Woods Hole.) Within ten years, the United States Fish Commission ordered a special steamer, the USS *Albatross*, the first vessel constructed specifically for marine research. Equipped with dredging devices and laboratory space to prepare specimens, the *Albatross* explored fisheries and marine resources along both coasts, the Caribbean, and as far north as the Bering Sea.

The general public was also interested in what lay deep below the sea's surface. Since the 1830s, Victorian holiday travelers had been encouraged to take up collecting shells, marine life, and sea weeds; exploring the beach and coastline was considered a wholesome activity, suitable for women and children. Both men and women naturalists published books about the natural history of the seashore, stimulating an interest in what lay farther out at sea. The inventive French writer Jules Verne added to this enthusiasm with his 1870 adventure novel *Twenty Thousand Leagues Under the Sea*, which imagined explorers in an electrically powered submarine traveling through a colorful underwater world while carrying out advanced marine biology studies.

Verne hit on something that many scientists—and the public—dreamed of: seeing life in the deep firsthand instead of hauling it to the surface. Since the early eighteenth century, inventors had experimented with designs for diving suits that would allow humans to roam the ocean's depths—primarily in hopes of retrieving gold and silver bullion from ancient wrecks. (In the 16th century, Leonardo da Vinci imagined one of the first diving suits—not for the purpose of exploring life in the deep but for attacking enemy ships.) But devising a suit with flexible joints that would remain watertight at depth and yet not seize up under pressure proved challenging. Finally, in the 1920s, a German firm succeeded in developing several atmospheric diving suits, equipped with bubble- or bucket-shaped helmets, that allowed salvage workers to descend below 220 feet. Most of the suits were equipped with a hose and a regulator to deliver pressurized oxygen on demand from a surface supply, and a kind of umbilical cable that tethered the diver to his ship. All were stiff, heavy, and awkward to use. Outfitted divers looked like a cross between knights in full body armor and today's mechanical robots. While some divers succeeded in retrieving the hoped-for precious metals, they weren't able to do much exploring of life in the deep.

Inventors, often engineers or mechanics, had also spent recent decades dabbling in submarines and submersibles, and, by the 1920s, had created vessels capable of descending to nearly 400 feet below the surface. These early submarines lacked windows, however, and so were useless for observation; their main purpose was to attack an enemy's ships. The field took a giant leap forward in the 1930s, when William Beebe, then America's most famous naturalist, decided to tackle the problem. At the time, he was known primarily as a flamboyant ornithologist, explorer, and lecturer, and for his award-winning popular books about his adventures capturing birds for New York's Bronx Zoo, where he was a curator.

A man of insatiable curiosity, Beebe had studied ornithology, geology, and paleontology at Columbia University but never earned a degree. This did not stop him. Thanks to his infectious enthusiasm for birds, he was invited in 1889 to become an assistant curator of ornithology at the newly opened New York Zoological Park (later renamed the Bronx Zoo). Beebe took his first research trips to Nova Scotia to study, collect, and photograph birds. By 1903, the twenty-six-year-old scientist had published so many articles and photographs that he was elected to the American Academy of Sciences. He led bird collecting and exploring trips to Mexico, British Guiana, and Brazil, becoming a specialist in tropical ecology and, ultimately, director of tropical research at the zoo. But Beebe began to dislike killing birds, even for museum collections, and became an ardent conservationist.

In the 1920s, Beebe's attention turned to the sea. In 1927, at age fifty, he led a diving expedition to Haiti and Bermuda, using a diving helmet and dredges to explore marine life. But neither method gave him the view of deepwater organisms that he yearned for. He'd grown to believe that animals could not be fully understood unless studied in their ecosystems—the places they inhabited. The idea, new for its time, influenced many younger scientists, including the eminent ant researcher E. O. Wilson, the great ecologist Rachel Carson, and famed marine explorer Sylvia Earle.

For his tropical forest studies, Beebe advocated methodically documenting all organisms that lived in a small area of wilderness—a standard method now in ecology. He'd received permission from the British government to do the same thing in the waters off Nonsuch Island, Bermuda, where he established a research station in 1928. From here, he intended to study the animals inhabiting an eight-square-mile area of ocean, from two miles below to the surface. At first, he thought he could accomplish this by diving and dredging, but he soon realized these methods were inadequate.

Beebe began to dream of an underwater exploration device, like a diving bell, which he could sit in and use to descend into the world below. The *New York Times* carried articles describing his plans, which caught the attention of an independently wealthy engineer, Otis Barton, an admirer of Beebe's, who had been working on a submersible device of his own.

The two men began to collaborate, improving on Beebe's initial idea. In 1930 they tested the first bathysphere, as they called their rotund cast-steel submersible, off Bermuda, making a short, shallow dive. After additional tests, manned and unmanned, they were finally ready for a deep dive. The two men climbed inside their invention and somehow managed to fit their large frames into a space not much bigger than a dog kennel. They waited for the crew to fasten the exterior bolts, sealing them inside, and next felt the sphere lurch as a crane hoisted it above the deck of their ship; they felt their invention hit the water and watched as bubbles streamed past the one viewing porthole while they sank into the deep.

The bathysphere was not navigable; it remained tethered to the ship on a stout cable throughout their dives. They quickly broke records: at 550 feet, reaching a depth no person had ever managed previously, and watched as the sun's light grew increasingly faint. At 600 feet, the water took on a mystical shade of blue that Beebe described later as "the blueness of blue." Finally, the machine reached a depth of 800 feet, where no sunlight penetrated. They were the first men ever to enter this dark world. Holding a handkerchief to his mouth and nose so that his breath would not fog the window, Beebe could "peer out and actually see the creatures which had evolved in the blackness of a blue midnight," as he would later write in his bestselling memoir *Half Mile Down*. Instead of the badly damaged and shredded marine organisms he'd seen in his dredging devices, Beebe now spied intact animals going about their everyday lives. The difference was like switching from black-and-white still photos to color movies, and he reveled in the animals' "colors and absence of colors, their activities and modes of swimming . . . their sociability or solitary habits."

Beebe and Barton made improvements to their submersible and continued to set diving records, finally descending in 1934 to the half mile below the ocean's surface that would give Beebe's memoir its title. They had little time to linger in the deep. They were ordered back after only five minutes; the captain feared the winch might have trouble bringing the bathysphere to the surface. On another dive to nearly the same depth, Beebe arranged a real-time radio broadcast on NBC via a telephone cable attached to the bathysphere's main cable so that Americans could listen to his descriptions of life in this dark world. At 1,800 feet, far "below the level of humanly visible light," he could just make out coiled deep-sea snails, strangely compressed hatchetfish, and unidentified "schools of fish, all brilliantly lighted."

Many deep-sea organisms use biochemical reactions via a light-emitting molecule to create bioluminescence. They flash or glow in the dark like fireflies, not to see but to attract prey or mates, or to hide, or to scare away predators. At 2,200 feet, Beebe saw a silver-dollar-sized light explode in a shower of bioluminescence; most likely, this was a species of shrimp (*Parapandalus*) that produces a glowing cloud of sparkling lights when frightened, similar to the inky mist octopuses eject when frightened or escaping a predator.

Beebe's and Barton's dives landed them on the front pages of newspapers around the world, making them "celebrities as big as rock stars," according to Beebe's biographer Brad Matsen. For an article in *National Geographic*, which sponsored some of his dives, Beebe worked with an artist named Else Bostelmann to illustrate the wondrous creatures he'd seen. The feature and drawings further stimulated the public's appetite for knowledge about deep-sea life. However, in his broadcast and in his books, the scientist struggled at times to find the words to describe all he'd seen. "We need a whole new vocabulary, new adjectives, to describe adequately the designs and colors of [life] under the sea," he wrote in frustration at one point. He'd been similarly exasperated by the limits of technology on his dives and longed for "telescopic eyes which could pierce the murk." The bathysphere's porthole afforded a narrow view of the world below, which stretched tantalizingly for "hundreds of miles . . . over so much of the world," nearly all of it unexplored.

Beebe's broadcast and popular writings inspired many others to explore the tropical forests and oceans. His and Barton's bathysphere also pushed inventors around the globe to tinker with the design. Others soon created diving vessels that were more easily navigable, including one that, in 1960, dived with two men on board to a record 35,814 feet in the Pacific Ocean's Mariana Trench. Innovators also worked on doing away with the heavy and cumbersome hardware that helmeted divers used. In 1926 Yves Paul Gaston Le Prieur, a French naval officer and inventor, had developed a self-contained underwater breathing apparatus (SCUBA) that allowed the diver to carry air tanks on his back, freeing him to swim. But the flow of air was poorly regulated: the diver could remain underwater for only a few minutes and thus was restricted to shallow dives.

What divers really needed was an air supply that entered their lungs at the same pressure as the surrounding water—a tricky problem because the pressure increased dramatically the deeper they went. So divers needed a valve, or regulator, that would respond automatically to the pressure around it. Finally, in the early 1940s, French navy diver Jacques Cousteau and engineer Emile Gagnan invented just such a device as well as an autonomous diving suit. With the "aqualung," as Cousteau called the invention, he and his diving pals became "menfish": humans who could swim in the ocean with the ease and comfort of whales and fish. On his first dive using the aqualung, off the French Rivera in June 1943, Cousteau, who would become another beloved popularizer of the deep sea, descended to sixty feet, trying out somersaults, loops, and barrel rolls. "I stood upside down on one finger and burst out laughing," he wrote later in *The Silent World*, an international bestseller. "Delivered from gravity and buoyancy, I flew around in space. . . . I reached the bottom [about sixty feet down] in a state of transport. A school of silvery sars (goat bream fish), round and flat as saucers, swam in a rocky chaos. I looked up and saw the surface shining like a defective mirror. In the center of the looking glass was the trim silhouette of Simone [Cousteau's wife], reduced to a doll. I waved. The doll waved at me."

Spying some dark crevices in the rocks below him, he swam into what proved to be a small cavern. Lobsters covered the ceiling. Cousteau plucked a few from the rocky roof and carried them to the surface for lunch with Simone.

With that dive, Cousteau and his diving friends knew they had changed our human relationship with the sea forever. "From this day forward, we would swim across miles of country no man had known, free and level, with our flesh feeling what the fish scales know."

Over the next three months, Cousteau and his partners logged five hundred dives with their aqualungs—making deeper and deeper descents as they sought the limits of their bodies and equipment. They used a knotted rope to track how far below the surface they could go, ultimately diving to 130 feet. After World War II ended, Cousteau carried out underwater research and mine clearing for the French navy, setting a new depth record for a free diver: 300 feet under the sea. He also used his scuba equipment for underwater archaeology, exploring a sunken Roman wreck off the coast of Tunisia.

Much like Beebe, Cousteau was eager to share the deep-sea world with the public. He took a leave from the navy to make underwater films with the backing of a wealthy British politician and philanthropist, Thomas Loel Guinness, who purchased a former car ferry, *Calypso*, and leased it to Cousteau for one franc a year. Government grants and appeals to manufacturers for free equipment helped him outfit his ship and hire a crew.

Cousteau filmed in color: porpoises, sharks, octopuses, manta rays, and flashy fishes, the water all brilliant blues and inviting greens. He captured mysterious, spooky grottoes from which moray eels sometimes emerged, and ghostly shipwrecks draped in sea dust and seaweed.

He and one of his diving partners, Frédéric Dumas, also wrote about their underwater adventures in *The Silent World*. Published in 1953, it was an overnight hit and remains popular today, with more than five million copies in print in twenty-two languages. In the book, Cousteau and Dumas don't shy away from detailing the dangers of ocean life, nor their own imprudence. All of the first sharks they met, including one that was twenty-five feet long, fled from them in fright—which "led us to a foolish negligence," Cousteau wrote. "[W]e were ready to state flatly that all sharks were cowards." They felt so safe that they harpooned a bottlenose dolphin to use as bait to draw the sharks close for filming, only to find that the sharks—including that twenty-five-footer—were more interested in Cousteau and Dumas. Soon they were encircled. Only with luck did the men, "weak and shaken," make it back to their ship.

Cousteau was not a trained scientist, and biologists sometimes mocked his observations as amateurish. But he was more astute than they realized. After watching a large group of what he called harbor porpoises (which were most likely dolphins, as porpoises don't vocalize at a frequency we can hear) swim through the Strait of Gibraltar, he deduced that the animals were navigating using echolocation. Cousteau had heard the dolphins' "mouselike squeaks," and noticed that they always knew where they were and how to find the strait, a "ten-mile gate . . . in the immense sea." It seemed they must be "equipped with sonic or ultrasound apparatus by which their squeaks give them the feel of unseen bottom topography." Cousteau was one of the first to suggest that cetaceans (not just bats) had this ability.

Working with a young French film director, Louis Malle, Cousteau turned his years of footage into a documentary, which he gave the same title as his book. When *The Silent World* (the underwater world is actually not quiet at all; it simply sounds that way to human ears) was released by Columbia Pictures in 1956, only a handful of people had seen what Cousteau had witnessed, and the general public hungered to view this world themselves. Most had only a vague idea of the wild spectacle of life that resided in the deep. Beebe's books and articles had given them some hints, but Cousteau's color movie revealed the underwater world in an entirely new, almost palpable way, and people flocked to the film. At the 1956 Cannes Film Festival, *The Silent World* was awarded the Palme d'Or, making it the first documentary to receive this honor; Hollywood added to the movie's kudos with an Academy Award for Best Documentary.

Cousteau would go on to produce two more Oscar-winning documentaries and a hugely popular television series, *The Undersea World of Jacques Cousteau*, which ran on ABC from 1966 to 1976 and made him a celebrity in most American homes. Speaking in French-accented English and wearing his red beanie as he explored the world's oceans aboard the *Calypso*, Cousteau revealed the ocean and its bountiful organisms to millions of households. When ABC canceled the show, the marine explorer found a new home for it with the Public Broadcasting Service, which renamed it *The Cousteau Odyssey* and aired it from 1977 to 1980. His programs won forty Emmy Awards.

Marine explorer, inventor, filmmaker, and conservationist, Cousteau educated millions about the oceans and sea life—and inspired their protection. He was a member of the National Academy of Sciences, served as director of the Oceanographic Museum of Monaco for thirty years, and created the nonprofit Cousteau Society in 1973 to preserve and protect the marine environment. In his later years, he was showered with awards: in 1977 the United Nations awarded him the International Environmental Prize; in 1985 President Ronald Reagan gave him the Presidential Medal of Freedom; in 1988 the National Geographic Society bestowed its Centennial Award on him; and in 1989 he was elected to the Académie Française, a centuries-old council.

Cousteau may not have been educated as a marine biologist, but he inspired thousands of young people to explore the world beneath the sea. "We all owe a debt to Cousteau," said Susan Farady, a specialist in marine policy and law, and previously director of the New England office of the Ocean Conservancy, a nonprofit conservation organization. For Cousteau's passion, inventions, and discoveries led to the dawn of marine biology's golden age.

4

William Beebe's illustrated articles in *National Geographic* and Jacques Cousteau's technicolor documentaries on the wonders of the marine world cemented in the midtwentieth-century popular imagination the idea of an "inexhaustible sea" full of treasures for the taking. But since at least the nineteenth century, fishermen in the United Kingdom have feared that the ocean's supply of fish might, in fact, be limited. They'd seen their trade increase with the industrial revolution, and while that had meant good business, by the 1860s, the fishers grew concerned that the populations of cod, herring, and mackerel were dwindling. In Scotland, traditional fishers who relied on handlines and longlines for their catches were particularly alarmed by two newer techniques: drift netting and ring netting, which had been introduced in the 1830s and were believed to catch undersized fish indiscriminately.* The United Kingdom Fishery Board banned these practices in 1851 and enacted other rules about the size of fish that could be landed. Nevertheless, fishers worried that their catches were diminishing, and so they asked the government, Was it possible to exhaust their fisheries?

In response, a Royal Commission on the Sea Fisheries was convened in 1863. During the next two years, the commissioners interviewed fishers in 127 fisheries around the United Kingdom and in 1866 organized a meeting to report their results. Thomas Henry Huxley, a comparative anatomist best known for his unwavering support of Charles Darwin's revolutionary 1859 book *On the Origin of Species*, and one of the commission's officers, reported that the fishermen's fears were unfounded. He and the other commissioners cited a number of reasons for their skepticism: first, the oceans were enormous, and while some areas might be overexploited, there would always be others of equal productivity that hadn't been fished yet; second, people caught so few fish compared

---

* Actually, by the mid-1850s traditional fishing methods had already adversely affected the stocks of commercial whitefish according to a new analysis that concludes "the most likely reason for this decline is the rapid intensification of fishing from open boats using the traditional techniques of handlines and longlines."

with other predators that humans couldn't possibly affect fishes' population size; and finally, fish were astonishingly fertile—indeed, the egg production of a single female could offset a large catch. And since fishermen could fish wherever they wished, they could simply move to other fishing grounds if they encountered a depleted area. The depleted areas would then recover naturally. There was thus no need for any fishing regulations, and the commission recommended removing existing laws.

But the fishers' worries persisted. Finally, at the 1883 Great International Fisheries Exhibition in London, one of the world's fairs that were popular in the latter half of the nineteenth century for showcasing the achievements of the attending nations, a conference was called to discuss some of the more serious matters affecting the fishing industry. Huxley, now the president of Britain's Royal Society, the world's oldest independent scientific academy (founded in 1660), was invited to give the inaugural address. This time he differentiated among fisheries, noting that it was wise to control those found in rivers, such as salmon fisheries, and those involving shellfish, such as oyster fisheries, because people could catch all the fish or strip an oyster bed clean. The same, however, was not true for fish in the sea.

"I believe . . . that the cod fishery, the herring fishery, the pilchard fishery, the mackerel fishery, and probably all the great sea fisheries are inexhaustible," Huxley told his audience. "That is to say that nothing we do seriously affects the number of fish. And any attempt to regulate these fisheries seems consequently . . . to be useless."

It was Huxley who coined the term "inexhaustible sea," and the phrase stuck in the scientific imagination for much of the next hundred years. But the biologist had not foreseen the effect that steam-powered fishing vessels would have on people's ability to catch staggering tonnages of fish. In 1855, fishers on schooners off the coasts of Maine and Newfoundland landed 7,800 metric tons of cod using the old technique of bait attached to hooks. When mechanized trawlers dragging enormous mesh nets replaced these line fishermen, their hauls increased exponentially, topping out at nearly two million metric tons by 1970. Fishers caught cod at every level of the sea and every stage of life, as well as the prey fish the cod ate. It was not sustainable. The sea's supply of cod had lasted five hundred years and provided a good living for Newfoundland fishers but by the end of the twentieth century, the cod were depleted. The Canadian Ministry of Fisheries and Oceans outlawed cod fishing off the coast of Newfoundland in 1992. Despite the moratorium, which is still largely in effect, the cod have not yet recovered.

Much the same thing happened to the sardine fishery off of California in the 1930s when trawlers were having a heyday bringing in tons of sardines to be canned on Monterey's famed Cannery Row. While the rest of the country suffered through the Great Depression, the bayside city's sardine industry boomed. More boats joined the fishing fleet, and more canneries were added every year. In the last boom year, from 1936 to 1937, more than seven hundred thousand tons of sardines were landed off California. And then the fish disappeared. In 1946 the fleet pulled in only fourteen thousand tons of fish; most boats came back empty.

Marine biologist Ed Ricketts who ran a biological supply house on Cannery Row, collecting and preparing specimens from the seashore, kept an eye on the sardine fishers in Monterey Bay. By 1946, Ricketts was warning that the fishermen were "taking too much fish." He expected the fishery to collapse. But biologists from the California Division of Fish and Game (now the California Department of Fish and Wildlife) had no authority, and federal biologists (who oversaw the offshore catch) had no management responsibilities for California. In fact, historians say the federal biologists were working to help develop the fishing industry and therefore looked for explanations other than overfishing to explain the sardines' decline—such as climate change.

There were attempts to regulate the industry, with some biologists even calling for a moratorium. But as Ricketts reported, the trawlers "refused to listen, selected their evidence [such as citing other scientists who would state that it was virtually impossible to overfish a pelagic species] . . . [and] always got their way." In a letter to the writer John Steinbeck, a friend of his, Ricketts was more blunt: "This year, with the sardine population perhaps at a record low, we have the greatest number of [canning] plants in the history of the industry, with a greater number of larger and more efficient boats than ever before, scouring the ocean more intensely than any time in the past. . . . [W]e can answer for ourselves the question 'What became of the fish?': they're in cans."

Ricketts tried to alert the sardine fishers and canneries to the cause of the problem by writing a front-page article for the annual sardine edition of the *Monterey Herald* in 1947. In it he explained how marine food chains work, and the connections between sea temperature, currents, and the ocean's productivity. Ricketts suspected that overfishing wasn't the only reason for the sardine shortage. A change in water temperature and the availability of plankton could also influence the numbers and distribution of the fish—which sometimes departed California's waters for regions farther south. In time, other marine biologists would confirm that shifting ocean currents do indeed cause the sardine population to fluctuate according to a predictable fifty-to-sixty-year cycle. But that was too late for the California sardine fishery.

However most populations of fish weren't disappearing as quickly as the Monterey Bay sardines, and so in the years after World War II, the US fishing industry continued to expand. A belief in the sea's unlimited bounty held. Francis Minot, the director of the Marine and Fisheries Engineering Research Institute, in Woods Hole, Massachusetts, even coauthored a 1954 book titled optimistically *The Inexhaustible Sea*. According to him, the ocean's bounty "extends beyond the limits of our imagination." In 1964 the annual global catch totaled about fifty million tons, and a US Interior Department report predicted that the catch could be "increased at least tenfold without endangering aquatic stocks." Only three years later, the department revised its estimate upward: the catch could be increased to two billion tons a year, enough to feed the world's population ten times over. Even in the 1990s, US policy was based "on the belief that the ocean's productivity was almost limitless," noted Michael L. Weber, an NMFS advisor, in his 2002 book *From Abundance to Scarcity: A History of U.S. Marine Fisheries Policy*.

But the peak of the world's catch had already been reached. It topped out in the late 1980s at about eighty-five million tons, about two billion tons below the Interior Department's overly exuberant estimate.

Thus, marine biology, a field that began as one of adventure and discovery, quickly became devoted instead to conservation and management. The commercial fishing industry now relies on marine biologists to maintain the remaining wild fish stocks. Fishery specialists are charged with determining the overall health of fish populations—gathering data about the sex, size, weight, and condition of the fish, and tracking their abundance and the number of adults and juveniles via annual trawl surveys—and calculating the rate at which they can be caught sustainably. Some marine biologists doubt this can be done at all, although the Alaskan pollock fishery has had some success. But even this well-managed fishery may not be immune from the total collapse that all seafood fisheries are expected to suffer, an event scientists expect will occur by 2050. These biologists worry that the loss of marine biodiversity worldwide has profoundly reduced the ocean's ability to produce seafood, resist diseases, filter pollutants, and rebound from stresses such as climate change and overfishing. Based on an analysis of historical, experimental, and fisheries data, as well as observational records of ocean species and ecosystems, the researchers predict that every species of wild-caught seafood—from tuna to sardines—will be

90 percent depleted by the middle of this century. Nevertheless, the scientists say there is hope. If we work to actively save marine biodiversity in all its forms, and restore all of our depleted fisheries worldwide, we can slow down and even stop the pending disaster.

"[M]AN . . . CANNOT CONTROL OR change the ocean as . . . he has subdued and plundered the continents," wrote Rachel Carson in her 1951 book *The Sea Around Us*. A decade later, she would write the classic *Silent Spring*, which explained the havoc pesticides such as DDT were wreaking on the environment and helped to spark the modern environmental movement. That's the book she's best remembered for today. But Carson started her career as a marine biologist—although she hated boats and could not swim—and *The Sea Around Us* was wildly successful, winning the National Book Award and spending eighty-six weeks on the *New York Times* bestseller list.

But, alas, Carson's hopeful quote wasn't true. The sea's vastness gave most humans the wrong impression: that it was indestructible. It wasn't, of course. Carson's own optimism lasted less than a decade. "[T]he belief that the sea, at least, was inviolate, beyond man's ability to change and to despoil . . . has proved to be naïve," the author stated in the preface to the 1961 edition of *The Sea Around Us*. It wasn't just that the fish that were dying off; governments were now burying the "contaminated rubbish . . . of the Atomic Age" in the sea, she wrote with undisguised horror and disgust. The practice continued through at least 1993, until international agreements banning it were reached. But the sea continues to be seen as a place to spill our refuse; recently, the US Environmental Protection Agency (EPA), established in 1970, approved the dumping of toxic wastewater from fracking offshore oil and gas operations into the Gulf of Mexico. It probably does not come as a surprise, then, to learn that by the birth of the modern conservation movement in the 1960s, humans had also been driving sea creatures extinct for centuries.

In 1741 a Russian ship, the *St. Peter*, was dashed to pieces on the shore of what is now called Bering Island, in the northern Pacific. The Danish commander, Vitus Bering, and twenty-eight of his crew soon died, partly from the effects of scurvy. The remaining forty-eight sailors were stranded for another ten months. They eked out a living hunting seals, seabirds, and sea cows—four-to-ten-ton mammals that grazed peaceably on the seaweeds in the coastal waters. George Steller, the ship's naturalist, observed that the sea cows appeared to be monogamous and lived in small family groups, with the adults working together to protect the young. The animals, relatives of the Indo–West Pacific dugongs, had inch-thick hides, and at first the men could not kill them even with their spears. Then one tried a harpoon, which did stick, and the crew hauled the sea cow to shore. The meat and fat were delicious, and likely helped save the men's lives.

Eventually the sailors managed to construct a boat from the remnants of their ship and rowed to safety, taking with them the pelts from sea otters they'd killed on the island. Soon other ships were searching Bering and the other Aleutian Islands for sea otters—while living off of sea cows. In 1768, not even thirty years after their discovery, sailors killed and ate the last Steller's sea cow.

The Steller's sea cow may have been the first large marine mammal humans drove to extinction, but it would not be the last. Hunting spelled the end for the sea minks that once inhabited the eastern coast of North America; they were exterminated by the beginning of the twentieth century. People also killed too many Japanese sea lions and Caribbean monk seals, both were eradicated by the early 1970s, and nearly wiped out the sea otter. In 2002 the last confirmed photo was taken of the baiji, or Yangtze River dolphin, a freshwater species; it is now believed to be extinct. And a mere dozen vaquitas—at five feet long, the world's smallest porpoise—survive in the

Gulf of California, the only place where they are found. By the time you read this book, the vaquita will likely be extinct. Until the late twentieth century, it seemed likely that many whale species would share these animals' fate.

Commercial whaling probably began in Europe during medieval times, although recent archaeological discoveries suggest that Romans may have hunted whales for profit some two thousand years ago. Basque whalers, from what is now Spain, dominated the European market from the eleventh century onward. They crossed the Atlantic in search of new whaling grounds in the sixteenth century and established whaling camps on the Labrador coast, where they hunted whales such as rights and bowheads.

When the Pilgrims arrived aboard the *Mayflower* at what is now the tip of Cape Cod, Massachusetts, in 1620, the sea was thick with whales. "We saw daily great Whales of the best kind for oyle and bone," they wrote, adding that they wished they'd brought the tools for whaling, such as harpoons. Eventually they did establish a whaling industry—and soon, of course, there were very few whales left. For the next two hundred years, whalers left New England ports to sail the world in search of their prey.

There were some species that even these professional whalers could not catch: finback (or fin) and blue whales, the latter the largest animal ever to grace the earth. Both were simply too fast for men in ships powered by sails and oars. But in 1868 these species lost their advantage when faster steam-powered catching vessels were introduced, and a Norwegian whaling captain invented an explosive harpoon that could be shot from cannons mounted on the bows of ships, making it much more efficient than earlier hand-thrown harpoons. Whaling was further mechanized some decades later with the introduction of factory ships. Now crews could haul killed whales onto deck, where men with flensing knives stripped off the flesh, instead of visiting whaling stations where this task was previously done; the blubber was rendered into oil in huge cookers below deck. A good crew could reportedly reduce a sixty-five-foot, fifty-ton fin whale to a pile of flesh and a few pots of oil in forty-five minutes. The remains were tossed into the sea.

Over the next decades, commercial whalers slaughtered three-quarters of a million fin whales and 360,000 blue whales in the Antarctic's Southern Ocean, the world's richest whaling grounds. As the populations of these giants decreased, hunters turned to smaller humpback, sei, and sperm whales, killing hundreds of thousands of each. They also killed more than a hundred thousand minke whales, a species once considered too small to bother with.

Whalers would seem unlikely conservationists. But by the 1940s, even they realized they needed to regulate their hunts or else drive the creatures extinct. In 1948 the major whaling nations established the International Whaling Commission (IWC) to oversee the sustainable management of the world's whale populations. The IWC set hunting quotas for each species, but over the next four decades, the numbers of most continued to decline—largely because the Soviet Union falsified its data. Between 1948 and 1972, the Soviets reported killing only 2,710 humpbacks, for example, when they'd actually slaughtered more than 48,000 in the Southern Ocean. The Soviet whaling fleets also killed great numbers of blue and right whales, severely depleting their numbers. Marine biologists believe the Soviet Union was also responsible for killing many of the remaining northern right whales in the eastern North Pacific, a population that remains so endangered it may never recover. By the 1980s, whalers had reduced the populations of some species by 95 percent or more.

Marine biologists had been warning since the 1960s—a potential loss that caught the public's attention as the environmental movement began to take hold. People had become increasingly aware of cetaceans' intelligence, largely through John Lilly's work with bottlenose dolphins. A controversial figure, Lilly was a neurophysiologist who became captivated by the impressive size and abilities of cetacean brains.

"The sperm whales have brains six times the size of ours," he wrote in his 1967 international bestseller *The Mind of the Dolphin: A Nonhuman Intelligence.* "Before they are annihilated by man, I would like to exchange ideas with a sperm whale. I am not sure they would be interested in communicating with me because my brain is obviously so much more limited than theirs." His popular book led to the idea that dolphins and whales had higher mental abilities than ours as well as mystical powers, which we humans might tap if we learned to communicate with them. Although much of Lilly's research was discredited, some science historians think his work and writings did more to transform our relationship with whales than that of any other scientist.

The public became even more enamored of whales after Roger Payne, originally an ornithologist, and Scott McVay, an English literature major without scientific training who had worked with dolphin researcher John Lilly for a few years in the 1960s, published in the journal *Science* in 1971 their discovery that male humpback whales sing. The US Navy had recorded the songs on hydrophones while tracking Soviet submarines; a naval engineer at a station in the Bermudas gave some of the recordings to Roger Payne (then a young biologist studying bird and bat calls) and his wife, Katy, a researcher in acoustic biology at the Cornell Lab of Ornithology. Katy Payne converted the whales' sounds into spectrograms—images of their frequencies. (She was thanked in a footnote for her spectrographic work.) While working with Lilly, McVay had learned to analyze spectrograms of dolphin calls, and applied his skills to the humpbacks' sounds, as did Katy Payne; their analysis showed that the whales' wails, squeaks, and moans contained rhymes— distinct phrases and themes that were repeated at intervals, much like human music. A year before the *Science* article was published, Roger Payne also released an album of field recordings, *Songs of the Humpback Whale*, which remains the bestselling natural history recording of all time. In 1977 some of the whales' choruses were included on the gold phonograph record (which was meant to epitomize the variety of life on Earth) carried aboard the *Voyager 1* space probe on its journey into deep space.

Magazine articles in *National Geographic*, *Natural History*, and *Audubon*, and television wildlife programs kept the giant mammals in the news, and soon the cry "Save the Whales" appeared on bumper stickers, T-shirts, and flyers across the country. The outcry grew after the environmental organization Greenpeace (dedicated originally to reducing nuclear weapons testing in the oceans) decided to make saving the whales its next great cause. In 1975 the group confronted a fleet of Russian whalers about to harpoon a pod of sperm whales off the coast of California. The Greenpeace crew zoomed up on their orange Zodiacs, placing themselves between the hunters and the whales. One of the whalers fired his harpoon toward the activists, but it sailed safely over their heads. Footage of the encounter was broadcast around the world. It was the first time in human history, commentators noted, that humans had put their lives in danger to save a whale. "[T]hat was the moment that launched the modern ecology movement," recalled Greenpeace founding member Rex Weyler in 2015.

Cetacean biologists and activists began pressuring the US Interior Department to recognize the large whales as endangered. They played the humpback whale recordings at government hearings, as well as at an IWC meeting in Stockholm, building more public opposition to the whaling industry. These concerns led Congress to pass the Marine Mammal Protection Act of 1972, which prohibits killing and importing to the US marine mammals or their products.

Finally, in 1986 the IWC member nations banned the commercial hunting of whales—something that had never before (and has not since) been done for any other group of animals.

While some whale populations have recovered in the three decades since, others, such as northern right whales, remain on the edge of extinction. Bowhead whale populations are still small and vulnerable, as are those of the western gray whales off the coasts of Japan and Korea. And while a handful of nations, such as Iceland, Norway, and Japan, continue to have limited hunts, none seems interested in returning to the days of unregulated slaughter.

As whale populations have recovered, IWC member countries have relied on cetacean experts to report on their condition, providing new and necessary research opportunities. But many questions remained unanswered: Where did the creatures live? What foods did they consume? Where and when did they give birth to their young? How far could they dive below the surface? What were their societies like? And how could we protect them from ship strikes, refuse, entanglement, pollution, and other dangers of living in a human-dominated world?

Robin Baird was one of the young marine biologists eager to supply answers.

5

In 1987, when Robin Baird started the fieldwork for what would become his PhD thesis, he was building on nearly fifteen years of data that other scientists had collected on the killer whales off Canada's Vancouver Island. Although orcas are a cosmopolitan species, inhabiting every ocean from the Arctic to Antarctica, these Pacific Northwest animals were the first to be studied as living individuals. In the decades before Baird, pioneering researchers concentrated on what they termed the "resident" killer whales, which numbered around 350 and lived in two communities. The scientists called those living in Johnstone Strait at the northern end of the island the northern resident community, and those that lived in Haro Strait to the south, the southern resident community.

Thanks to Michael Bigg's research, every whale in these pods was known to the scientists, who could recognize them from the unique scars and markings on their dorsal fins and backs, and their gray-white saddle patches. The researchers assigned a letter to each pod and a number to each animal. Thus, the first orca they learned to recognize was called A1. But the biologists also had names for the whales. They called one with a pronounced nick in her dorsal fin Nicola, and another whose dorsal fin had been nearly amputated in an accident Stubbs. During his university years, Baird had volunteered with Bigg and added photos to the marine biologist's killer whale ID catalogs.

The scientists could distinguish the pods from one another by listening to their calls via hydrophones: microphones used for listening and recording sounds underwater. Each pod, they discovered, had a discrete dialect and accent, as determined by analyzing their calls via spectrograms. Some of the whales' sounds are so distinctive—rising or falling whistles and squeaks—that people can also recognize them just by listening. Such variations are now recognized in the calls and songs of many other mammals and birds. Perhaps most remarkably, these calls remained stable over time. For instance, the dialect the J pod uses today is almost identical to what it used in 1958, when the Royal Canadian Navy made the first known recording of these orcas' sounds.

When the scientists began researching the orca populations off Vancouver Island, the myth of the fearsome killer whale still lingered in the popular imagination. Many orcas bore bullet scars from fishermen who'd shot at the whales because the fishers thought they were eating too many fish or were simply dangerous; indeed, one in four captured killer whales to later die in captivity were discovered to have bullets lodged deep in their bodies.

But public perception of killer whales was beginning to change, thanks to "celebrity" orcas such as Skana at the Vancouver Aquarium, Namu at the Seattle Marine Aquarium, and Shamu at SeaWorld in San Diego. The day that Moby Doll, the very first captured orca, was introduced to the public by the Vancouver Aquarium in 1964, some twenty thousand people turned out to see him—the same number that attended a Beatles concert in Vancouver's Empire Stadium a month later, at the height of Beatlemania. Watching the beautiful panda-colored animals up close, and, as the years passed, learning from scientists about orcas' intelligence and gregarious natures, altered people's attitudes. "Killer whales ceased being demonic bringers of death, all teeth and vengeance, and almost magically became transformed . . . into cuddly water-going pandas," one journalist observed.

Despite the public's adoration, many of the most famous orcas had short, sad lives. Poor Moby Doll lived only eighty-eight days in a net pen at Pender Harbour, north of Vancouver, dying from wounds he'd received when captured, as well as from starvation; his minders didn't know that he ate only fish until *two months* into his captivity, when someone offered him one; he then consumed up to two hundred pounds of fish a day. Moby Doll's death was chronicled in newspapers from Vancouver to London, where the *Times* gave his obituary a two-column heading, "the same size given to the outbreak of World War II," noted conservationist Erich Hoyt in his history of the species, *Orca: The Whale Called Killer.*

Because so many people had thronged to see Moby during his brief life in captivity, the Vancouver Aquarium and others across the globe paid for more orcas to be captured and put on display. Between 1962 and 1973, 247 killer whales were seized from the waters off Washington and British Columbia. Of these, 12 died during the capture, mostly by drowning in nets, while 53 were sold to aquariums—16 of which died during their first year on display. The others managed to escape or were released.

These captive orcas sparked public interest in their wild kin. People eagerly joined orca-watching cruises, and the whales (highly social animals that they are) often readily approached the dozens of boats soon taking tourists into the waters off Vancouver Island, swimming alongside to peer at the passengers—even though some of these orcas had seen humans capture or shoot at their family members. The public bought marine researchers' books and attended their lectures, keen to stay abreast of the orcas' family histories and comings and goings. People were advised to refer to the killer whales as orcas, after their Latin name, *Orcinus orca*, because the resident pods ate only fish—primarily chinook salmon. If we call them "killer whales," said Paul Spong, a neuroscientist and cetacean expert from New Zealand who worked with Skana at the Vancouver Aquarium for two years, then we should refer to ourselves as "killer apes."

Spong and other marine biologists who worked with the captive orcas acknowledged that they learned a great deal about these animals by studying those in captivity. But the more they learned, the more some scientists felt that seizing whales in the wild was wrong. Spong said so, and was soon out of a job at the Vancouver Aquarium. But to the public, who loved the orcas, he and other marine biologists who spoke up in defense of them were heroes. By the mid-1970s, public opinion had changed, and while people still enjoyed watching orcas leap and dive at SeaWorld, they no longer thought they should be captured in the wild.

The final capture in Washington State waters took place in 1977 close to Olympia, the state capitol, where lawmakers were discussing making the Salish Sea an orca sanctuary. As news of the capture spread, people lined the streets of Olympia in support of the bill. It passed, and by the 1980s, the orcas living in the waters between British Columbia and Washington State had become iconic symbols of recovering whale populations worldwide—a triumph of the environmental movement. Sadly, though, these orcas are now nearing extinction because dams and fishing have greatly reduced the populations of their primary prey, chinook salmon.

RESEARCHERS SUCH AS PAUL Spong, who championed the rights of orcas in newspapers and on the radio, are one reason that when laypeople today think of marine biologists, they often picture scientists who study whales. But although "Save the Whales!" had become a rallying cry of the environmental movement, cetacean researchers in the 1980s still had many unanswered questions. It seemed, for example, as Bigg had first observed, that two types of orcas lived in the waters near Vancouver, and that they were socially and reproductively isolated from each other—an extremely unusual situation for any mammal. A third type living farther offshore (and therefore called "offshore orcas") only added to the confusion when it was discovered in 1988.

The presence of three large predatory marine mammals that lived close together and looked essentially alike— although they exhibited somewhat different behaviors, such as the size of their pods, and where and how they hunted— puzzled the marine biologists. Most evolutionary biologists of the time argued that new species originated when some geographic feature separated a population. It might have been a mountain range or a large river or desert. If the animals were unable to meet to mate, they were likely to develop genetic changes over time that would continue to keep them apart. If they became reproductively isolated from one another— meaning that they could no longer have viable offspring— then they would be considered new species.

Many biologists were of the opinion that a new species could not evolve without geographic separation. And for large animals that freely roamed the ocean, such as orcas, it seemed highly unlikely that such a separation could happen. All orcas, regardless of where they lived, were therefore classified as members of one species.

Yet here in the narrow ocean straits of the Pacific Northwest, cetacean researchers regularly saw two distinct populations of resident orcas and orcas that were different from these two groups. The scientists had first encountered these nonresident whales in the 1970s, and were unsure what to make of them. Unlike resident pods, which could be reliably found in certain parts of the straits at specific times of year, and which traveled predictable routes as they foraged for fish, these other killer whales appeared randomly and seemed to wander aimlessly through the shallow bays and inlets. While the resident pods were typically made up of ten to thirty closely related individuals, these whales were rarely seen in groups of more than three or four, and these "ratty little groups," as Bigg called them, never spent any time with the resident whales. Bigg and his colleagues wondered if these wandering whales were simply passing through or if they were perhaps social "outcasts" from larger resident pods—similar to nomadic African lions that are pushed out of their prides. Deciding that these strange orcas were "in transit" to other locations, the scientists labeled them the "transients."

The transients had a distinct look, with sharply pointed dorsal fins and saddle patches that extended farther forward; they also lacked the black coloring that sometimes intruded on the white saddles of the residents. In addition, they differed from the strictly fish-eating residents in their dietary preferences, hunting marine mammals—including minke whales, Dall's porpoises, and the calves of gray and humpback whales. It was because of this sort of behavior that killer whales had gotten their name: they were literally killers of whales, a term (*asesinas da ballena*) coined by eighteenth-century Basque whalers who witnessed orcas tearing tongues and lips from dying or dead baleen whales. In 1862 a Danish zoologist confirmed that some orcas dine on marine mammals, when he reported on the stomach contents of a twenty-three-foot-long male found dead near Denmark. Before expiring, the animal had consumed thirteen porpoises and fourteen seals—and not a single fish. Although there was no evidence that orcas hunted humans, people realized the predatory mammals probably could. More than one hundred years on and halfway around the world, Bigg and his colleagues, including Robin Baird, watched transient orcas pursue and kill harbor seals. When the scientists examined the stomach contents of two transient males found dead on Vancouver Island, they determined one had devoured two harbor porpoises, a sea lion, and some twenty harbor seals (based on the remaining body parts) over an unknown period of time. The other's stomach contained a harbor seal, the feathers of an aquatic bird, a cormorant, and pieces of baleen from a gray whale. Although some scientists would continue to argue that the transients probably ate fish, too, most accepted Bigg's conclusion that these orcas dined almost exclusively on marine mammals. Occasionally, they apparently seized seabirds as well.

The mammal-eating transients differed from the residents

in another important way: while the residents were talkative, uttering whistles, pulsed calls (short, scream-like sounds), and echolocation clicks, the transients were largely quiet— probably, the scientists suspected, because they were essentially big game hunters and took care not to tip off potential prey. Like the residents, they had unique call repertoires, but the transients' weren't as broad and lacked the variation in dialects. Still, the transients' calls likely helped the whales identify one another and maintain their social bonds.

This was nearly all that was known about the mysterious transient killer whales when twenty-four-year-old Robin Baird began his master's program in the Ecology Department of Vancouver's Simon Fraser University in the fall of 1988. The whales offered the young scientist a golden opportunity to make his mark on cetacean research. But that would happen only if he could spend time with these notoriously difficult orcas every day. Transients "tend to be hard to find and, once found, they are easy to lose," cetacean biologists John K. B. Ford and Graeme M. Ellis wrote in their 1999 book *Transients: Mammal-Hunting Killer Whales*. Finding them, they added, was more a matter "of good fortune than good tactics, and staying with the group long enough to collect useful identification photographs and behavioral data can be quite challenging."

The transients stealthily and silently hugged the shore-line. They traveled erratically, intermittently speeding up and slowing down. And when they dived, they often vanished for more than ten minutes before surfacing to catch a breath—whereupon they were apt to vanish again. They also were less friendly to whale watchers and researchers than the resident whales were, typically evading approaching boats.

Baird knew all of this. He'd already spent two years collecting data for Bigg's research project, following and photographing the transient killer whales that hunted in Haro Strait and Juan de Fuca Strait, the areas between southern Vancouver Island and the Olympic Peninsula and US San Juan Islands. But now, as a graduate student, he had to approach the orcas with a different mind-set. It wasn't enough to document individual animals and record each one's behaviors. He had to ask *why* the resident and transient killer whales behaved so differently. What was it about hunting fish that led the residents to live in large, chatty social groups? Why did the transients live in smaller pods? The transients ranged farther afield than the residents did, but they also kept close to the shoreline. Why was that? What were the whales' foraging techniques in these shallow waters, and how did this affect their social behavior and reproductive success?

To answer these questions, Baird needed to find and follow the shy transients every day. His study area encompassed 1,358 square miles (3,000 square kilometers) off the southern tip of Vancouver Island, an area far too vast to patrol alone. Baird needed eyes on the water to help him, and so he devised a plan similar to the one Michael Bigg used to carry out the first orca census in the straits. Bigg had established a network of hundreds of volunteer observers who would telephone or radio whenever they spied killer whales. As soon as a call was received, Bigg or one of his team would race out to the location to photograph the animals. That was how he'd succeeded in collecting data on nearly every resident orca, and many of the transients.

Baird now organized his own informal "sighting network," as he called it. He gave his home phone number to fishers, captains of whale-watching vessels, local lighthouse keepers, and owners of waterfront properties. If they saw groups of killer whales swimming close to the shoreline, he told them, please call him at once. He also listened to a marine VHF radio while at home in case any vessels reported seeing orcas. Baird's girlfriend, Pam Stacey, was also involved in the research, so these daytime calls didn't disrupt his home life. As soon as he heard of a sighting, he dashed from their apartment in Victoria to the dock where he kept his boat, a five-minute drive. "I went out in a rapid-response sort of way whenever I got a report," he recalled, "and on really, really good weather days, I'd just head out early, after dawn, scouting and hoping to find whales."

Baird ran a lean operation. He used a small, soft-bottom, inflatable Zodiac borrowed from the university and carried his few supplies—notebook and microcassette recorder, camera and film—in dry bags stashed inside a plastic milk crate. He used the notebook to jot down basic information, such as what time he set out and the direction, and the recorder for all of his observations. Speaking them rather than writing them down let him always keep his eyes on the water and the whales. He dressed simply in a bright-orange Mustang Survival suit and fingerless gloves, and kept his binoculars at the ready, hanging from a cord around his neck. Often, Baird's advisor, Larry Dill, joined him, as did one of a number of curious undergrads. They were there to help get the boat on the water and to observe the orcas.

"Robin was absolutely focused on the work," Dill recalled. "So much so that he didn't want to stop to eat. In fact, he never did. For the whole boat, all he had was a box of Ritz crackers and peanut butter and Diet Cokes. I brought salami. You had to eat while we traveled because he wasn't going to stop. That focus was admirable, but it could make him appear to be an *asshole* too."

Some of the student volunteers "loved him," Dill said, and others despised him. Baird knew that his intense dedication to his research irritated people, but he couldn't change—at least, not during those early years. "I knew what I had to do [to collect the data], and I did that," he said candidly. Even now, "I don't like wasting time when I'm out on the water." Asked if his style as captain has changed over the years, he replied simply, "I'm a recovering asshole."

During his first two years as a master's student, Baird took five courses at Simon Fraser, requiring him to spend a couple of days a week at the university; otherwise he was in Victoria doing or analyzing his fieldwork. If he needed reference material, he could use the Simon Fraser library when he was there or the one closer to his apartment at the nearby University of Victoria.

"I'd worried that Larry would force me to take lots of statistics courses," Baird recalled, "but he said, 'No, they're not that important.'" Dill felt that knowing *how* to do statistics was far less important than knowing *why*. "Statistics can help you understand what you're thinking about," Dill explained to Baird, "but they can also mislead you." You might find something that appeared to be statistically significant but was actually "biologically irrelevant." Thus, biologists might take measurements from ten thousand specimens of northern fur seals and find significant trends in their length over time. But if the difference in length is merely a centimeter, it likely does not have any biological significance; that is, it would probably not affect the seals' reproductive success or numbers. Statistics were important for a marine biologist to know, Dill emphasized, if for no other reason than to recognize when you were being led astray.

After two years, pleased with the data his student was collecting, Dill moved Baird into the PhD program, where he could focus on his research, spending every day out on the water if he wanted. Robin was finding that the transient groups were not as difficult to locate as older researchers had reported. Knowing that the animals disliked the company of boats, Baird approached them carefully, often shutting off the motor and simply riding the swells, trying to be as unobtrusive as possible. "If we were too noisy, we'd interfere with their hunting," he explained. "As long as we just followed quietly beside or behind them, they largely ignored us." He, Dill, and the day's student assistant would divide the tasks: Baird drove, while talking into his recorder about the whales' behaviors, and the others took photographs or helped by tracking the pod. Baird recorded each whale's sex and estimated size, the pod's location, and, if a hunt was under way, the type of prey the pod was pursuing, so that its caloric value could be calculated later. He described the whales' behavior from the moment the subjects were first visible until they swam off—or low light, rough conditions, or dwindling fuel forced the Zodiac to return to shore.

For six years, Baird hunted the hunting whales, logging 434 hours of observations of twenty-six transient social groups, most of which were encountered on multiple occasions, and three of which researchers had previously never observed. He watched as the whales nosed around the inlets and rocky haulouts where harbor seals mated and birthed their pups; and as others explored deeper waters to chase harbor porpoises and the occasional seabird. Elephant seals turned out to be "probably their preferred prey," Baird told me. "They are the easiest to catch in relation to how much energy the whales have to use to catch them. Harbor seals are a close second." Dall's porpoises proved to be trickier prey, rocketing through the water at speeds as high as twenty-five miles per hour, although Baird found the orcas could match the smaller mammals' speed, making these chases "extremely exciting to watch . . . with the whales often completely clearing the water" in pursuit. Sometimes they even rammed the porpoises, tossing their prey into the air, and then, catlike, playing with the injured animal, letting it go and chasing it again.

Still, the transients rarely pursued porpoises, as the cost of the chase wasn't worth the small meal. For the same reason, the transients seldom hunted the small minke whales and migrating gray whale calves that were also abundant in the straits. But of the 136 attacks on seals that Baird recorded, 130 were successful. The harbor seals were largely defenseless. The only way they could protect themselves was to avoid being detected. If a pod spotted a seal close to shore, the seal sometimes escaped by staying in water too shallow for the whales to follow or hauling out on land. Knowing that seals were the transients' surest meal, the odd, wandering behavior that other scientists had reported now began to make sense. Although the seals' rocky haul-outs made up less than 1 percent of Baird's study area, the transients spent more than 12 percent of their observed foraging time nearby and made 35 percent of the kills Robin witnessed in the vicinity. The transients would nose around the haul-outs as they followed the shoreline's contours, circling rocks and islets in search of seals that might be hiding near shore. Baird's analysis showed that pods with only three killer whales were the most successful at this type of hunting, partly because they were quiet, and these whales ate the most food. (On average, a transient ate one and a half harbor seals every twenty-four hours of observation.) This explained why the transients were seen most often in small groups.

In deeper waters, however, Baird found that the transient killer whales lived in larger groups of five to eight. These pods regularly pursued porpoises as well as seals, and therefore needed more members so that they could take turns in swift pursuit. Larger groups also provided more opportunities for learning courtship, mating, and parenting skills; consequently, these pods tended to have more calves and juveniles. The smaller groups remained small because youngsters dispersed once they were old enough to mate, although it was unclear if they joined other pods or formed their own. In this, too, the transients differed from the resident orcas, in whose pods the mother was the leader, and all of her children remained with her throughout their lives.

In both large and small transient pods, the killer whales shared their prey with one another—something the fish-eating residents did not do as often. In one instance, Baird and his crew watched an adult female in a transient trio kill a juvenile harbor seal; twenty minutes later, they spotted her still carrying the intact carcass in her mouth. Suddenly she flicked her head and passed the body underwater to one of the other two killer whales: her adult son. (A transient female's firstborn son usually remains with his mother for life.) He carried it for a minute and then let it drop from his mouth as the third whale, his four-year-old sister, caught it in hers. They continued to pass the seal back and forth several more times until at last "the two adults came together and tore the seal apart," Baird wrote later. All three then dined on the shredded carcass. When finished, they set off on another hunt.

Often after such feasts, killer whales would stop for a while and engage in social behaviors, Baird learned. Usually silent, the transients would leap skyward, breaching the waters before falling back into the sea with percussive blasts. They leaped, cartwheeled, and smacked the surface waters with their tails—exuberant displays that Robin interpreted as indicative of being healthy and well-fed.

Baird's thesis, which he completed in the summer of 1994, provided additional proof that the resident and transient killer whales kept to themselves and did not mate with one another. He even documented an instance of resident orcas attacking one of the small three-member transient pods. The doctoral candidate speculated that in the distant past, there had been one species of killer whale in the Pacific Northwest that fed on both fish and marine mammals. But when these orcas encountered the abundant salmon runs, some groups began eating only fish. Over time, the two types of killer whales diverged further, each pursuing a different prey that required specialized hunting and dining techniques. While Michael Bigg had speculated that the "transients are probably a separate race of killer whale" from the residents, Baird went one step further, arguing that due to their distinct diet, genetics, and behaviors, they "should be considered as incipient species—that is, in the process of speciation."

Larry Dill, Baird's mentor, was pleased with the results. "He showed why the transients' social groups are so different from the residents," the professor told me, still proud of his former student. "And he showed that there was a group size for the transients that maximized the potential of every individual. If the groups were any larger, then all the members would suffer; that was why males left the group to mate and why the transients traveled in such small pods. Their foraging techniques drove all of their social behaviors."

It was new and noteworthy research, and in 1996, Baird published a chapter of his thesis, "Ecological and social determinants of group size in *transient* killer whales," in *Behavioral Ecology*, a leading scientific journal.

6

Robin Baird was awarded his PhD in August 1994. And like many young people with a new doctorate, he wasn't quite sure what to do next. He needed to find a way to "get paid to continue doing what I'd been doing," but he wasn't sure what type of paying job would fulfill his dream of "studying whales in the wild." He'd talked to his advisor and other faculty members about becoming a professor or working as a research biologist with Canada's federal Department of Fisheries and Oceans—two common careers for marine biologists. Both positions would assure a steady income, but they had drawbacks, too. As a government scientist, he would be working on projects the agency deemed important, leaving little time for his own research. A faculty position, Larry Dill warned, would require him to spend at least half his time on teaching and administrative tasks. Teaching held no appeal, especially with the added burden of bureaucratic paperwork. "It was stuff even my profs really didn't want to do," said Baird. "If you're spending fifty percent of your time doing things you don't want to do in order to do the things you want—well, it wasn't the kind of trade-off I was interested in making." These days though, twenty-five years on in his career, that's pretty much what he does—since he's responsible for writing and administering the grant proposals, while also writing up the research results for publication, reading other scientists' papers, and preparing for lectures and conferences. It's what happens, he said, when a scientist is successful in leading field projects.

Baird loved British Columbia and the camaraderie of the cetacean scientists there; he'd thought he would probably stay near Vancouver, studying whales for the rest of his life. But soon after graduation, he started to consider abandoning killer whales and switching to raptors, specifically Harris's hawks—midsize birds of prey known for their cooperative hunting style—a shift made possible because his specialty was behavioral ecology.

"I thought about taking the questions I'd asked about the killer whales and applying them to other species," Baird told me. He brought up the idea with Larry Dill, who "reminded me of how much time I'd already invested in the field studying cetaceans. He said it would make more sense to build on that knowledge than to have to get up to speed on a different group of animals and another ecosystem. It was good advice."

Another cetacean biologist, Stephen Leatherwood, whom Baird had met at a marine mammal conference in Miami some years before, had also cautioned him not to switch species. But if he did make the leap, Leatherwood recommended that Baird not do so entirely. "He thought I should maintain my reputation for being an expert on a particular system rather than working on many different systems and species, and not being an expert in any of them."

Baird decided to stick with killer whales. But there was a problem: he had no money. He was jobless, had student loans to pay off, and he'd maxed out his credit card. When he skipped a few payments ("not something I would encourage anyone to do"), the credit card company took away his card. "I was largely unemployed," he said, "and getting letters from collection agencies."

Toward the end of finishing his thesis, Robin had applied for a postdoctoral National Sciences and Engineering Research Council (NSERC) grant at the University of British Columbia—a common step toward an academic career. Whereas most US postdoc grants are awarded based on proposals by faculty advisors looking for assistants, this one would allow the postdoc to do whatever research he or she wished, based on a proposal to work with a particular advisor. The NSERC postdoc is the equivalent of a US postdoc from the National Science Foundation, the government agency tasked with supporting research and education in all nonmedical fields of science and engineering. The NSF pays a scholarship or stipend to the candidate, while the university provides office space. But any funding required to carry out the research must come from other sources.

Baird hoped to obtain sufficient funds to further investigate whether transient and resident killer whales were already two species or merely in the process of becoming two. He'd proposed the idea that they might already be separate species in the epilogue to his thesis, but after further research, he still wasn't sure. He also wanted to study the transients' diving behavior in greater detail.

For part of Baird's thesis, he'd modified an existing time-depth recorder (TDR) tag so that he could study killer whales as they dived and foraged below the surface. These tags were noninvasive: instead of attaching them surgically to the animal, Robin used suction cups to keep them in place. Once affixed, the tag recorded and stored data about the depth of the orca's dives and the time he or she stayed below before resurfacing. Baird successfully attached tags to one transient killer whale and six residents, using the resulting data to show how the two types differed in how they foraged and used their habitat. Additional data on the animals' diving styles would, he believed, bolster his argument for two distinct species of killer whales.

Robin fully expected to receive the grant. His credentials were solid: he'd already published a number of peer-reviewed articles (including, for the *Canadian Field-Naturalist*, status reviews of some dozen species of whales and dolphins, assessing their populations' health and distribution). He'd also helped establish and co-ran both the B.C. Marine Mammal Sighting Program and the Stranded Whale and Dolphin Program of B.C., part of a voluntary whale-stranding network whose members documented whales that turned up on coastlines. Baird and others would identify the species, assess the causes of mortality, and collect tissue samples for other studies, such as genetics and diet. "This work led to a number of publications in peer-reviewed journals," he said, "as well as yearly reports to the IWC." It was how he'd learned about Dall's and harbor porpoises, as well as false killer whales, and gray, minke, and beaked whales.

He also served as a research associate at San Juan Island's Whale Museum. The position didn't pay, but the title helped when he applied for grants. (Understanding how beneficial an impressive title can be for young marine biologists, Baird provides similar titles to some of the people who volunteer at Cascadia Research Collective and are actively engaged in research projects there.) But his hoped-for postdoc did not come through. "It was a bit of a blow," he admitted.

But Baird did not despair. A good friend and fellow marine biologist recommended him to a local School for Field Studies, which hired him as a junior instructor. (SFS, a nonprofit academic institution, teaches environmental courses at sites worldwide.) With his friend, he cotaught two monthlong summer undergraduate level courses on killer whale ecology to college students, and, in the fall, a marine mammal field course at the SFS program in La Paz, the seaside capital of the Mexican state of Baja California Sur. The La Paz program lasted three and a half months, and his students were all Americans. Baird was being paid in US dollars and hoped to save some of his earnings to pay off his debt. But after teaching the first of two planned semesters, he quit SFS and took a position to work on research with graduate students at Centro Interdisciplinario de Ciencias Marinas (CICM), a Mexican university laboratory, which paid him in pesos. (He spoke English with his students.) Unfortunately, a week later, the peso was devalued and dropped 30 percent in relation to Canadian dollars. Still, he stayed. "I didn't have many options," he said. "And it was a character-building experience.

It opened my eyes to the diversity of the world and made me realize I had more options than I'd realized. It convinced me that I didn't need to stay and work in BC the rest of my life."

Teaching was beneficial to him, too. As a shy person, Baird found public speaking awkward at first, but with practice, he "discovered how to entertain and inform people." It's something he thinks "every scientist should be forced to do, preferably when young," so that they can also learn how to "effectively communicate their results to the rest of the scientific community." In Robin's opinion, scientists who don't hone this skill "are just wasting time and money. I think scientists have an obligation to make their results available to the general public, not just through scientific papers, since so much of science is publically funded or has strong relevance to the environment."

Most of the funding for the fieldwork he'd expected to do with CICM dried up by April 1995, and Baird headed back to British Columbia to look for work. He searched the job postings on email lists from the Society for Marine Mammalogy and the Ecological Society of America's ECOLOG, as well as on MARMAM, an influential Listserv that he and Dave Duffus started in 1993 at the University of Victoria. And even though Robin didn't think a university career was the right path for him, he did apply for faculty appointments—

but only those that weren't primarily teaching positions and only at schools located along the coasts. He also took advantage of shorter-term projects, often as a volunteer, and for the next year lived a fairly peripatetic life. Baird worked on a Canadian Department of Fisheries and Oceans research ship for a month as it sailed north from Vancouver Island to the Queen Charlotte Islands, helping to spot seabirds and whales, and as a naturalist on cruises between BC and southeast Alaska. Then he was off to Dunedin, New Zealand, for an all-expenses-paid five-week trip to study bottlenose dolphins for the University of Otago at the invitation of scientists there who wanted to use his TDR tags.

Baird's tagging research was highly regarded, as it gave researchers a view of what whales and dolphins were doing underwater and where they were traveling. "Sometimes, when the water is clear, you can see them down to about five meters [sixteen feet] below," Baird explained, but mostly scientists see the animals only when they surface to breathe. Furthermore, he added, "You can't see them at all at night. I wanted to know what they're doing when they're not at the surface."

Baird hadn't invented the TDR tags. In 1989 a cetacean biologist named Jeff Goodyear had come up with the original design for attaching tags to wild whales with suction cups; he used these tags to track the nighttime behavior of humpback, minke, fin, and right whales. A few other scientists, including Mike Bigg, relied on more conventional radio-tagging methods, but these required researchers to capture the animal and surgically implant the tag—a technique that often resulted in complications. While working on his dissertation, Baird read about Goodyear's method and wrote a letter to the researcher at the University of Guelph—some two thousand miles away in Ontario—only to discover that Goodyear had moved to Victoria, where Baird lived. "So we met for coffee," Baird said.

Goodyear helped Baird design a tag for killer whales. They used his original design—including the $2 suction cups, made for car roof racks, to keep the tag attached to the whale. Following Goodyear's advice, he hollowed out the interior of a block of synthetic foam that could remain buoyant at depths of 1,000 meters (3,200 feet) and fitted the interior with a time-depth recorder, a VHF transmitter, and added weights, so that when the unit fell off the animal, typically after a few days, it would float with its antenna above the water. The VHF would transmit a signal that could be picked up from several miles away, allowing scientists to retrieve the tag and access the data on the animal's diving behavior, habitat use, and speed, as well as light levels and water temperatures.

These were exactly the kinds of details that marine biologist Karsten Schneider wanted to gather on a resident pod of bottlenose dolphins that lived in the dark waters of New Zealand's Doubtful Sound. Schneider, whose University of Otago supervisor had met Baird at a marine mammal conference and knew about his tagging work on killer whales, invited Baird to help him attach the tags—a not unusual invitation among marine biologists, who often collaborate on projects.

Using a crossbow or long pole, Schneider and Baird attempted to tag the dolphins as the animals traveled slowly near the bow of their boat. But while the orcas Baird had worked with for his thesis did not react strongly when hit, the Doubtful dolphins immediately tried to dislodge the tags, making vertical leaps or swimming away at high speed. After three days, Schneider and Baird managed to tag ten animals, but five of the tags fell off, so the partial data were of little use. The tags also provoked unnatural behaviors: the dolphins that usually happily rode the bow wave of Schneider's boat stopped joining him; they "changed only slowly back to 'normal' over the next two months," Baird wrote later. He and Schneider concluded that "suction cup tagging of this population of bottlenose dolphins is not feasible," and that it would probably be better to use invasively attached tags that would stay in place for several weeks, allowing the animals to get used to the device.

Some might have regarded the tagging project as a failure, but Schneider and Baird did not. "All sorts of things don't work out as planned," Baird told me. "It's good to accept that!" It was a lesson Robin had learned when working on his thesis. "I did all sorts of things that were going to be chapters of my thesis," he explained, "and instead were small appendices or didn't make it in at all, as they didn't work out. Just part of doing science."

He also recognized that even a failure can have important—and publishable—results. In an article for *Marine Mammal Science*, Baird and Schneider reviewed scientists' efforts to use telemetry (the automatic measurement and wireless transmission of data from remote sources) to study cetacean behavior, and noted that researchers could not assume noninvasive tags could be used on all cetacean species. At least other scientists could learn from their findings, disappointing though they were. And Baird had added another peer-reviewed journal to his resume. A strong list of publications can help "convince funding agencies you're doing good work," Baird explained, and thus assist in "getting support for additional work."

Baird did not linger in New Zealand. He'd been hired as a marine mammal and bird expert by Marine Expeditions, a Canadian tour company, and set off as a guide on an eight-day adventure from Ushuaia, Argentina, to the Antarctic Peninsula. "There is a lot of value in traveling and working with different species, seeing the variety when you're young," Baird advised. While Stephen Leatherwood's counsel about maintaining a sustained focus on one species stayed in the back of his mind, Robin also discovered that he gained insights into killer whales' behavior by branching out. "I've found that doing only one thing—say, studying only the songs of humpback whales—limits a person's creativity," he told me. "You get a broader view and richer understanding if you work with different species and do different things."

Baird continued to search for a position that would be right for him. "There were jobs," available, he knew; "the question was whether it was one I wanted." He wrote another proposal for a NSERC grant, and this time emailed cetacean scientist Hal Whitehead about taking him on as a postdoc. Whitehead was just becoming known for his brilliant mathematical approaches to studying the social structures of whales. Baird had met him at various conferences and was familiar with his work. To Robin's joy, Whitehead, who'd read some of the younger scientist's publications, agreed to let Baird join his lab. His reasons for picking the young marine biologist over other qualified applicants were practical: "I always prefer to choose people who will be comfortable at sea, and Robin had plenty of sailing experience," Whitehead told me.

When Baird headed to Whitehead's lab at Dalhousie University in Halifax, Nova Scotia, in the summer of 1996, Whitehead was starting his ninth year of study on the north-western Atlantic sperm whales. He was particularly interested in how the whales' societies had evolved and what held their pods together. Originally from England, he'd received his first degree in mathematics but switched to studying cetaceans after encountering a minke whale while sailing solo along the Nova Scotia coast. "Studying whales allows me to make a living while sailing," he said as we talked by phone. Although he claims not to be "a very observant person" and has difficulty identifying whales he's previously seen and photographed, Whitehead knows math and statistics and how to use these to better understand whales' populations, societies, and behaviors. For instance, when his mentor, biologist Roger Payne, who in 1967 discovered the songs of humpback whales, thought that southern right whales in the windy waters off Patagonia were using their broad tail flukes as sails, Whitehead told me that he'd figured out the "physics of how the whales move." Payne published his discovery about the sailing whales in *National Geographic* in 1976.

At Dalhousie, Whitehead launched a sailing program to

collect data on whales nonstop. He'd done his PhD on the humpback whales of the northwest Atlantic, working mostly from shore, but by the time Baird arrived, he was collecting most of his data while aboard a forty-foot oceangoing sailboat, the *Balaena*. "We follow whales in real time," Whitehead said. "It's physically and mentally debilitating. We work twenty-four hours a day for ten days to three and a half weeks, collecting data on the whales' social organization, behavior, and acoustics. It is wet and cold, and the food is bad. Most students don't have much experience with that kind of thing. Some realize when they get back to shore that they never want to do it again. And others love it."

Baird was among the latter. There was usually a team of five to six scientists, primarily graduate students and postdocs, on board to crew the *Balaena* and carry out the research. Each one handled a four-hour watch every twelve hours, shifting their watches so that "no one got the benefit of sleeping through the whole night. We all took turns cooking, too," Baird recalled. "There was an ice chest with a block of ice in it, and that melted fairly quickly, so by the end of the trip, our food options were very limited." Water was in short supply, too, and the scientists took only a "sailor's shower"—a single bucket of fresh water—once a week. Despite the privations, the *Balaena* journeys remain among

Baird's favorite experiences. "It's one you know you can never repeat," he reflected. "Each was so unique. We saw such a variety of seabirds and whales—Sowerby's beaked whales, northern bottlenose whales, fin whales, long-finned pilot whales, striped dolphins—most new to me. Many nights we put a hydrophone in the water as we sailed, so we heard the calls of the bottlenose whales and echolocating sperm whales all night long."

Baird had planned to join only one of Whitehead's trips but ended up sailing on five, all of which traveled to the Gully, the largest underwater canyon in eastern North America, which lies about 125 miles (200 kilometers) off the coast of Nova Scotia. Some 8,200 feet (2.5 kilometers) deep, it offers a variety of habitats—from the shallow terrace of land known as the continental shelf, to the deep ocean floor—and is a haven for endangered northern bottlenose whales, a gray, sausage-shaped species with bulbous foreheads and projecting, cylindrical beaks. Baird had seen stranded beaked whales, a closely related species, on Vancouver Island, but here he had the opportunity to work with living ones.

Northern bottlenose whales are one of twenty-three species of beaked whales, all known for their lengthy, deep dives. Cuvier's beaked whales can descend more than 6,561 feet (2,000 meters) below the surface and remain there for

Northern Bottlenose Whale

more than two hours, feasting on squid. These precise details weren't known yet when Baird began his research on the
species, but the northern bottlenose whales were suspected
of having extraordinary diving capabilities. So Baird and a
colleague, Sascha Hooker, tracked their dives in the Gully by
attaching suction cup tags to the animals' dorsal fins.

As he had in New Zealand, Baird shot the device from a
crossbow or leaned over and used a long pole to tap whales
that had quietly surfaced near his boat. The impact startled

the whales, as it had the New Zealand dolphins, but this time the animals soon settled down and continued their normal behaviors. Hooker and Baird collected sufficient data on their dives to write publishable articles, lengthening his resume.

Despite his five trips aboard the *Balaena*, Baird and Whitehead were never at sea together. With young children at home, Whitehead had begun turning over his usual role of skipper to graduate students. But the two scientists did see each other at Whitehead's lab. Baird had a desk just outside Whitehead's office, and Whitehead, he said, "would wander over from his office and run ideas past me. He was just developing his ideas about the culture of whales and in the process of developing his software programs for analyzing animals' social structures." So many people had been asking Whitehead to help analyze the social data they'd collected on various species that he decided to create SOCPROG (Programs for Analyzing Social Structure, a series of programs available to anyone online), so they could analyze their data on their own.

"In a postdoc, you want to develop different ideas and a different set of skills than what you did during your PhD," Baird said. "And that definitely happened for me in Hal's lab. You actually find several of his papers in mathematical journals."

For three years, Baird researched beaked whales and killer whales through his postdoc with Whitehead. Since Baird had raised his own funding, he chose what he wanted to study, and it was a productive time for him. His finances were somewhat more stable, too: he'd finally paid off his credit card bill, and begun paying down his student loans, and no longer received threatening letters from creditors. But his long-term career plans remained uncertain. He continued to apply for faculty positions but wasn't making much headway.

Then one day in early 1998, the phone on Whitehead's desk rang. Hal wasn't around, so Baird answered, as he often did.

"This person—a man—was calling from Hawai'i," Robin recalled, "and by the end of the call, he'd offered me a job as research director of a whale organization there. Now, Halifax is a lovely city, but I was envisioning my third winter there." He shivered at the memory. "I told him I'd think about it."

7

When the Maui-based Pacific Whale Foundation contacted Baird in early 1998, he listened with interest to the director's offer. The nonprofit, founded in 1980, is known for its educational ecotours, cetacean research, and conservation programs. As Robin recalled, the man on the phone "promised me total control of the project, identifying and collecting data on Hawai'i's cetaceans, including bottlenose dolphins and false killer whales"—the latter an intriguing, little-studied species. Equally enticing, the project had a budget of $250,000. But Baird knew, too, that it was best to investigate such a plum offer, so he started asking around. Some contacts, Robin said, told him the foundation's director "had a very bad reputation, and that in spite of what he'd said, he would try to exert complete control." Others, though, claimed the man "had mellowed" in recent years.

Baird was now in his midthirties. He'd come to enjoy his itinerant lifestyle, one he found made him the object of envy

False Killer Whale

of many of the older clients on the trips he led as a naturalist, which he continued throughout his postdoc for the extra cash. "They often said to me, 'I only wish I'd done what I wanted to do when I was in my twenties and thirties, like you are,'" Robin recalled. He was seeing the world and studying a variety of cetacean species, fulfilling the dream he'd had when he first turned to marine biology as an undergraduate. Still, Baird yearned not so much for stability but for an important, ongoing project—something along the lines of what Whitehead had achieved in Nova Scotia. In the end, he decided to accept the Pacific Whale Foundation's offer to lead the project; at the very least, he'd be working with new species, and, not insignificantly, he wouldn't have to suffer through another Halifax winter. Robin applied for a one-year, renewable work visa—although he thought it more likely he would stay only for six months.

Baird arrived in Maui on December 1, 1998, and soon settled into a small apartment near Maalaea Harbor, where the foundation's research boat—another rigid-hulled inflatable vessel was moored. "I started the project by doing what we're doing today," Baird said as we chatted aboard his boat while exploring the waters off the Big Island. "Just going out and looking for whales and dolphins and documenting our encounters."

The PWF project got off to a good start. Baird and two young research assistants photographed bottlenose dolphins and false killer whales, and began building a photo catalog of individual animals that would help the researchers spot their distinctive scars and markings. All seemed to be going well, and when the foundation asked Robin to stay on for another year, he agreed, although he'd found the director to be as difficult as he'd been warned. "But I was a fairly well-established researcher and could hold my own with him," Baird said. He liked living in Maui, too—not that he had any long-term plans to stay. He was unnerved when naturalists and assistants he met would say things like "I feel stuck here" because, Robin explained, "they weren't making enough money to leave."

WHILE WORKING FOR THE Pacific Whale Foundation, Baird occasionally heard some news snippets about Keiko, a killer whale and international cause célèbre. Keiko had been captured in Iceland two decades before. After stints in aquariums there and in Canada, he'd ended up on display in an entertainment park in Mexico City, where his pool, which was originally designed to hold dolphins, was a mere 114 feet long; Keiko was 21 feet long. After eight years suffering in the pool's warm, chlorinated seawater, Keiko was spotted by movie scouts searching for an orca to star in the 1993 movie *Free Willy*, about a boy's quest to free a captive killer whale. The movie was a smashing success, and afterward, Warner Bros. studio began helping with efforts to find Keiko a better home—a movement that soon turned into calls to "Free Keiko!" Environmentalist and filmmaker Jean-Michel Cousteau—Jacques's oldest son—founded the nonprofit Free Willy–Keiko Foundation (later renamed the Ocean Futures Society), which purchased Keiko and moved him to a new, custom-built pool in Newport, Oregon, where the orca began to regain his health.

"Keiko was probably not the best candidate to release into the wild," Baird said. The killer whale, captured when he was only a few years old, had been held in captivity for twenty years, spending most of that time alone or with a couple of bottlenose dolphins—a devastating experience for a highly social animal with strong ties to his pod. Most orca researchers doubted he would find or be allowed to reenter his pod if returned to Iceland—and he probably could not exist in the wild on his own. Released, Keiko would also pose a risk to wild populations, possibly introducing them to foreign diseases. Nevertheless, when the Ocean Futures Society, impressed by Baird's research on Canadian killer whales, asked Robin if he was interested in being involved with the effort to reintroduce Keiko to the wild, he said yes. For him, it was another research opportunity: he would learn more about the killer whales of Iceland, and he was curious about how Keiko's swimming abilities compared with those of killer whales in the wild.

He visited Keiko in Oregon in early 1998, while still a postdoc in Nova Scotia, to calibrate the swim-speed sensors on a tag the team attached to the killer whale's side. Baird then traveled to Iceland, where he attached the same type of sensors to wild orcas to find out how Keiko's swimming would compare to wild Icelandic killer whales and whether he would be able to keep up in their hunts for herring. The society reviewed the results and, spurred by public pressure, decided the reintroduction should go ahead. Keiko was flown to Iceland in a thirty-foot-long tank that September, three months before Baird was to move to Hawai'i.

After his first six months with PWF, Baird was due vacation time, which he used to travel to Iceland to work with Keiko for a couple of weeks in the summer of 1999. The orca was now being kept in a larger floating sea pen in Klettsvik Bay, on an island off the country's southwest coast. Here the whale could experience the cold waters of the North Atlantic and the sensation of fish swimming nearby. "I was involved in taking Keiko on 'walks,'" said Baird. The team of about ten people would open the orca's pen, and Keiko would swim out. A boat with observers, including Robin, led the way, while another vessel followed behind him. The daily walks let him become accustomed to the area gradually, all the while equipped with one of the suction cup tags to monitor his swimming and diving behavior. After each walk, Keiko dutifully returned to his enclosure.

Then one July day, a pod of orcas swam nearby, and the team decided to introduce Keiko to them. "It was his first exposure to wild killer whales," said Baird, "and he basically freaked out. He took off at high speed and traveled about forty kilometers [25 miles] from his pen." The crew stayed out on the tracking boat all night following Keiko, who eventually returned to Klettsvik Bay.

Baird stayed for a week or two, joining the team on a couple more walks, and Keiko had a few more encounters with members of his own species. "Sometimes he would socialize with wild killer whales, and other times he ignored them," Robin recalled. "But he never stayed with them, and never joined their hunts or fed in the wild." Baird's short-term role in Keiko's reintroduction to the wild ended upon his return to Hawai'i, but others continued the effort the next two summers. Keiko, though, never joined a pod; he lacked the social skills to do so, scientists involved with the project would later say. Sometimes he did meet other killer whales, but only floated motionless at the surface. He also never hunted or caught a wild fish, and never dived deeper than twenty-six meters (85 feet); wild killer whales spend most of their dive time between fifty and seventy-five meters (164–246 feet). After every trip out of his pen, he returned hungry because he had not fed. Then, in August 2002, he surprised his caretakers by migrating on his own to the west coast of Norway. There, however, he was found spending more time with boats and people, even allowing children to ride on his back. His caretakers moved to Norway and continued to care for him while trying to help Keiko become truly free. But he always returned to people for food and contact, and lived in an open sea pen, where he dined on his favorite frozen herring until his death in 2003 at the age of twenty-six or twenty-seven, probably from pneumonia.

AFTER HIS TRIP TO Iceland, Baird returned to Hawai'i to resume his work with the Pacific Whale Foundation. But as the months went by, he found himself increasingly at odds with the director. The foundation never seemed to publish any papers, which puzzled Baird, who thought it important to share one's research and data. Finally, he and the director had a serious dispute, and Baird quit.

Now he was unemployed and without an income in Hawai'i—a situation he'd wanted to avoid. But he also had data to analyze and papers to write, so he was actually happy to have a break. He hoped the network he'd gained in his months on Maui might help him get new paid contract work. He could not "just get a job," because he was on a TN visa, which is issued to people who have prearranged jobs. But he could work on a contract basis or with grant monies. So he quickly applied to the Hawaiian Islands Humpback Whale National Marine Sanctuary, which awarded him a contract to study humpback whales' diving and nocturnal behaviors. The Island Marine Institute, a local organization in Maui that wanted to support research, provided him with a boat and fuel.

Humpback whales, which can be found in all major oceans, were one of the most heavily hunted of the baleen whales. An estimated two hundred thousand were killed in the twentieth century, and some populations were reduced by 95 percent. To protect the humpbacks, the International Whaling Commission banned hunting the species in 1966, and the United States listed them as endangered in 1970. Shortly after the ban, marine biologists in Hawai'i began spotting humpback whales in shallow waters close to shore. Humpbacks were not known to visit the islands prior to this time—and it is still not clear to scientists what led these whales to Hawai'i. By the time Baird began his project, the visiting humpbacks numbered close to ten thousand—a sign that the protections were working and the species was recovering rapidly. The whales' resurgence is one of the great conservation success stories; most humpback populations were removed from the endangered species list in 2016.

Humpback whales visit the Hawaiian Islands primarily

during winter, traveling from their feeding grounds in the North Pacific to give birth, sing, and compete for mates. As scientists studied these newcomers, they concluded that the animals needed protected areas where they could engage in these activities safe from predatory killer whales—hence Congress's creation of the Hawaiian Islands Humpback Whale National Marine Sanctuary in 1992. These shallow protected waters around the islands are recognized as one of the world's most important habitats for this species. Baird's study would help the sanctuary's managers understand better how the whales were using the area—important data, since the US Navy was planning to expand its shallow-water submarine training range here and intended to install "sound sources," as it calls some of the equipment used for sonar exercises.

By now, Baird was quite familiar with the waters off Maui. He would depart the Lahaina dock on the island's west coast early in the morning several times a week to search for humpback mother and calf pairs, single singing adult males, and groups of males fighting for a single female's attention. (Female humpbacks choose their mates.) The competitive groups were the easiest to approach: sometimes there were as many as a dozen big males, all charging hard through the water. As soon as he spotted such a group, Baird motored within five to fifteen meters of his target animal, and shot a tag from his crossbow, a skill he'd acquired in 1992 first for tagging and later for taking biopsy samples (for genetic, disease, and other studies) with a dart, which removes a small amount of tissue. As always, he had eager helpers, who videoed the tagging attempts and the whales' reactions, and photographed their dorsal fins for identification. None of the whales reacted with the high-intensity leaps and breaches of the New Zealand bottlenose dolphins. Most continued whatever they'd been doing; for instance, one singing male flicked his tail and immediately resumed singing. Baird's study lasted two months, during which time he tagged fifteen whales and recovered fourteen of the deployed tags. The lost tag stayed on a traveling humpback that swam out of the study area, likely heading north.

Baird and his crew collected the recorded data on the tags, along with small amounts of skin cells that sometimes stuck to the inner surface of the suction cup; these were later used to determine the animals' sex via genetic analysis. They'd avoided tagging any calves or mothers with calves, and so ended up with thirteen males and two animals whose sex was not known. The males, especially those swimming in competitive groups, spent most of their time in the upper waters, but tagged whales also dived deep, traveling to depths greater than 328 feet (100 meters) about twice every hour; some even dived to the very bottom of the sanctuary's waters, about 600 feet (182 meters) down, a region which the navy's sonar would penetrate. Baird's study indicated further research was needed to see how these sounds might impact the whales. Although he did not yet know it, Robin would in time become a specialist on how the navy's submarine training programs affect cetaceans.

While searching for humpbacks, Baird also kept an eye out for other cetaceans, particularly rarer species such as false killer whales, pygmy killer whales, and dwarf sperm whales. No one was paying him to study these species, but in retrospect, he said, "It just made sense to collect any information about them that I could get. As a birder, it seemed like the obvious thing to do. Birders get excited when they see rare species." It's not just about adding a rare bird to their lifetime list. Birds appearing in habitats where they're not usually seen can indicate some environmental shift, such as a warming or wetter climate, or possibly the return of a species to a range it used to inhabit, perhaps because conditions have improved. Conversely, it may mean that a species has been pushed out of its habitat due to destruction, competition, or disease, and is looking for new, habitable territories. Or it may simply be that the bird has made a mistake or been blown off course. By recording such unusual sightings, birders can help scientists track avian responses to climate change or habitat loss, and alert authorities to help protect an endangered species.

The same possibilities applied to the whales and dolphins Baird was photographing. While most marine biologists thought these mammals were simply passing through the Hawaiian islands, making sustained study pointless, Robin thought there was likely some pattern to their movements. He didn't know what he would do with the data he was gathering in the short term—or long term, for that matter. But while he was on the water, he figured he might as well make note of what he saw.

8

By the beginning of the twenty-first century, one of marine biologists' primary research—and ethical—concerns was whale and dolphin strandings, especially after a horrific incident in the Bahamas on March 15, 2000.

Marine biologist Ken Balcomb was out for a morning stroll only a short distance from the home where he and his then wife, Diane Claridge, had lived for nine years, studying three species of beaked whales in the blue waters of Great Bahama Canyon off Abaco Island, when he spotted a Cuvier's beaked whale on shore. "What in the world are you doing here?" a puzzled Balcomb asked as he knelt beside the animal. It was not yet dead. Balcomb knew at a glance that this was a male. The cetacean's protruding teeth poked out and up like short tusks from its lower jaw, a trait seen only in males of the species, which use them to fight each other; their bodies are typically laced with scars from such battles. From the amount of scarring and the size of his teeth, Balcomb could see that the whale was young, too, which surprised him. Usually only elderly or sick whales heave themselves onto shore, perhaps because they are disoriented. Most stranded cetaceans do not survive.

The rotund, sausage-shaped animal lay in about three feet of water, his left eye mashed in the wet sand, his right eye focused now on Balcomb. The scientist rocked the whale to one side, searching for signs of injury, but saw only fresh scratches that had likely been caused when the cetacean crossed a nearby coral reef. Then he noticed deeper white rake marks and circles, as well as round holes in the whale's dorsal fin—the telltale scars of cookie-cutter shark bites. They formed a pattern that Balcomb recognized. Only two weeks before, he and Claridge had tracked this young male through three long dives off the island's South Point. They'd finally succeeded in getting a perfect photo to ID him and had given him the code Zc-34 in their catalog. Zc stood for the animal's scientific name, *Ziphius cavirostris*; he was number 34 in their catalog.

Balcomb set to work getting the whale back into its deepwater home. With his bare hands, he dug a trench beneath the creature, which filled slowly with water, and the biologist managed to push the cetacean into the sea. But just as it looked as if the whale would head deeper into the ocean,

Cuvier's Beaked Whale

he made a wide left turn and returned to the shore. As the morning progressed, Claridge and a group of volunteers joined Balcomb to help. Once again they pushed the youngster into the sea, but again he turned back toward the beach. The whale "was very confused," Balcomb said later and "kept making big left turns as we tried to move [him] into deeper water."

After several more attempts, the beaked whale finally dived and disappeared into the deep. While the team watched to make sure he didn't return, a fisherman in a small boat came into view, shouting that he'd just seen another whale stranded elsewhere on the island. Balcomb jumped into his nearby pickup truck and drove south to find the whale. About a mile from the first stranded whale, he spotted the second one, another adolescent male Cuvier's beaked whale. He was bleeding from coral cuts, and several sharks were circling offshore in anticipation of a good meal. Balcomb and the others managed to get the whale away from the sharks and back into the water. This one did not swim back to shore but, rather, dived into the deep waters of an offshore canyon.

But the team's apparent success at returning the two whales to the sea was overshadowed by reports that came in over Balcomb's VHF radio: two minke whales had just been found stranded on another island twenty-five miles to the southeast, and a Cuvier's beaked whale mother and calf were beached on a small cay, or low-elevation, sandy island, near Grand Bahama, sixty miles to the northwest. The calf was already dead.

Over the next two days, Balcomb and Claridge investigated reports of ten additional strandings: more beaked whales (eight Cuvier's, one Blainville's) and an Atlantic spotted dolphin. In June they discovered the badly decomposed remains of a Gervais' beaked whale, a seventeenth victim. Balcomb would eventually determine that all seventeen cetaceans came ashore almost simultaneously along a sixty-two mile (one hundred-kilometer) arc-shaped stretch. Volunteers managed to return ten of the mammals to the sea, but seven died, several of them bleeding from their ears. Balcomb and Claridge collected tissue samples, including whole heads, from six of these animals—material they hoped would help solve the mystery of why so many cetaceans of so many different species had thrown themselves out of the sea.

No one had ever witnessed this kind of multispecies stranding before; usually, in the Bahamas, one or two whales might beach themselves every year. But Balcomb already had a hunch about why this incident had occurred. The morning after finding the first beached whale, he arranged a surveillance flight. He wanted to look for other dead or dying whales—and for the likely cause.

Before becoming a cetacean researcher, Balcomb had spent five years as an officer in the US Navy, working in the Sound Surveillance System (SOSUS), where he became familiar with the use of sonar to detect passing submarines. On his surveillance flight that March day, he spotted three stranded whales—and a US Navy warship towing a large rectangular object. He asked the pilot to fly close enough so that he could videotape the ship.

Back at Balcomb's home, his assistant enlarged a freeze-frame image from the camcorder; Balcomb could just make out the destroyer's hull number. He typed it into the *Jane's Naval Weapons Systems* website and learned the ship was the USS *Caron*, packed with modern armaments, including antisubmarine helicopters. Very likely, Balcomb concluded, the navy was conducting war games in the area, probably within Great Bahama Canyon—the home of the beaked whales.

The Great Bahama Canyon is four miles deep, one hundred miles long, and fifty miles wide. The beaked whales of the Bahamas spend their lives in its waters, hunting squid, seeking mates, and raising their calves, often at depths a mile or more below the surface, where they can linger for more than an hour. Beaked whales are, like all cetaceans, acoustically sensitive animals. By sending out sonar clicks (which sound to our ears like buzzes) at very short intervals and listening for the return echoes, they can determine the size of the animal they're hunting and the speed and direction it's traveling.

The US Navy also uses sonar. In 1946 President Harry Truman established the Office of Naval Research (ONR) to invest in underwater research and antisubmarine warfare to ensure the nation's safety during the Cold War. One early area of investigation was whether dolphins and toothed whales use echolocation to hunt their prey. Donald Griffin, a Harvard University biologist, had revealed bats' sonar in 1940 through experiments that proved the flying mammals could navigate in total darkness by emitting ultrahigh-frequency sounds and listening for the echo—findings that surprised the military, which had only recently developed its own radar and sonar technology. Griffin invented the term *echolocation* to describe this ability and suggested that some cetaceans might also use sonar to hunt in the ocean's midnight-dark waters. The biologist would write later that "the notion that bats might do anything even remotely analogous to the latest triumphs of electronic engineering struck most people as not only implausible but emotionally repugnant." Dolphins and whales were another matter, though, since people (erroneously) regarded them as more akin to humans. And so the navy began pursuing the idea that understanding cetacean sonar might help improve man-made sonar.

In 1960 zoologist Ken Norris, a World War II navy veteran and curator of the newly opened Marineland of the Pacific, an oceanarium in Southern California, proved that bottlenose dolphins did indeed echolocate, using sound transmissions to see. Norris covered the eyes of captive dolphins with suction cups, temporarily blinding them, and turned them loose to find a scrap of fish in an underwater maze. But the dolphins weren't really blind, because they use sound to see—so, of course, they found the bits of fish. Building on Norris's discovery, other researchers demonstrated that dolphins' bio-sonar was far superior to that of the navy. Using a stream of clicks, the cetaceans could detect a tangerine-sized target three hundred feet (ninety-one meters) away. From that same distance, they could distinguish an aluminum plate from an iron one, as well as a hollow tube from a solid one, and ball bearings of microscopically different sizes—all in a cluttered and noisy marine environment. They accomplished this by emitting two thousand clicks per second, aiming and adjusting each individual click by altering its volume, frequency, and direction. If necessary, they could send out two click streams simultaneously.

Dolphins' echolocation abilities quickly became a hot area of research—much of it funded initially by the US Navy. The navy conscripted dolphins, beluga whales, and sea lions to serve as spies, underwater mine detectors, and possibly even assassins. Grants to military and civilian scientists helped lead to the development of marine mammalogy as a separate and legitimate scientific discipline. Even today the Office of Naval Research remains the primary source of funding for marine biologists and oceanographers around the world.

Thus, by the time Balcomb and Claridge found the stranded beaked whales in the Bahamas, the US Navy was well aware that many cetacean species rely on sonar for their daily activities. And yet the navy had never investigated what would happen to such sound-sensitive animals if they were blasted with jet-engine-like noises in their underwater homes—which is what occurs when vessels with hull-mounted devices emit sonar pulses into the sea to see if they'll ping off foreign submarines.

Some marine biologists suspected these sounds were causing trouble for marine mammals. In 1991 and 1998, scientists reported in the journal *Nature* on four unusual mass strandings involving beaked whales: three in the Canary Islands and a fourth in Greece. NATO (North Atlantic Treaty Organization) naval maneuvers had been under way prior to all four incidents. But the navy largely ignored these scientists' concerns.

Balcomb knew this history, and as luck would have it, a friend from his college days at the University of California at Santa Cruz was now in charge of the Office of Naval Research. Balcomb telephoned Bob Gisiner and told him about the strandings in the Bahamas. Gisiner apparently hadn't heard about the incident. At the end of their call, Gisiner said he would send the navy's best whale pathologist, Darlene Ketten, to the islands to help investigate. He didn't know if the navy had any exercises under way in the Bahamas, but he would try to find out.

Two days after finding the first stranded Cuvier's beaked whale, Balcomb began to wonder if any news of the event was being reported publicly. To find out, he turned to MAR-MAM, the marine mammal Listserv at the University of Victoria that Robin Baird had helped establish while a gradu-ate student. Neither the Bahamian government nor the US National Marine Fisheries Service nor ONR had posted even a brief announcement. So Balcomb did. He listed the loca-tion, discovery time, and species of every stranded cetacean his team had documented.

At the time, Baird was still the senior editor of MAR-MAM, and, he believes, "likely approved" Balcomb's post-ing about the mass strandings. He was still in Maui that March, having just finished his study for the Hawaiian Is-lands Humpback Whale National Marine Sanctuary and getting ready to take up a new position as the stranding co-ordinator for the NMFS in Beaufort, North Carolina—one of more than a hundred groups that coordinate volunteers watching for beached whales. Baird had often dismissed the idea of working for a government agency, but as a Canadian citizen he could work only as a contractor for the US gov-ernment.

As soon as he read the news, Baird, like Balcomb, sus-pected that navy sonar was likely involved; he'd read the reports in *Nature*. Curious to learn more, he used his position on the Committee of Scientific Advisors for the Society for Marine Mammalogy—which had invited him to be a member—to contact Roger Gentry, the head of the Marine Acoustics Department at the NMFS. Baird asked Gentry if the navy "could be responsible" for the whales' stranding. "Amazingly," Baird said, Gentry denied the possibility. But Robin wasn't persuaded. As summaries of Balcomb's reports began to appear in the general media, Baird noticed that the navy never denied having conducted some type of exercises on the north side of Abaco Island prior to the strandings.

There can be natural reasons for strandings. Some scientists have suggested that perhaps toothed whales and dolphins get confused when echolocating around gently sloping coastlines or during hurricanes. Or perhaps some species, such as pilot whales, are so social they simply follow one another onto the beach when one is ailing or confused. But strandings, especially mass events involving multiple species, have also become far more common in the late twentieth and early twenty-first centuries—suggesting that unnatural causes are also involved.

Thanks to the 1972 Marine Mammal Protection Act, when whales strand on US shores, the NMFS is required to investigate as part of the overall effort to conserve these animals and understand the threats they face from human activities. But until the Bahamas incident, the NMFS had never connected any cetacean deaths to naval exercises. In April 2000, five weeks after the Bahamas strandings, the navy finally acknowledged that US and foreign warships had traveled through channels north of the islands prior to the incident; the flotilla included seven surface vessels operating standard, tactical sonar in the midrange frequency. The navy did not yet say that its exercises and the whales' strandings were related—but more and more marine biologists had become suspicious, especially after Jim Mead, a curator at the Smithsonian Institution's National Museum of Natural History and a cetacean expert, surveyed the scientific literature from 1834 (when the first stranding was reported to a scientific journal) to the time of the Bahamas event and discovered fifty known mass strandings of beaked whales. Out of these, only six "involved more than one species," Mead wrote in a report for the Smithsonian, and "in all six events, there were naval maneuvers present in the area." Mead distributed his paper on MARMAM—a move that, as one observer noted, "upgraded the sonar threat to whales from an unsubstantiated rumor to documented science."

A year later, Balcomb and Claridge added to the literature

showing a direct link between naval sonar and whale strandings by publishing a report about the Bahamas incident in the *Bahamas Journal of Science*. Darlene Ketten, the NMFS whale pathologist, had analyzed the tissue samples and whale heads and sent the two biologists her results. Her findings, while preliminary, clearly revealed "injuries consistent with an intense acoustic or pressure event." Some months later, the NMFS investigators issued a final report on the incident, noting "significant cranial lesions among the beaked whales," although, interestingly, "not in a single delphinid," or dolphin. These hemorrhages were found "consistent with impulse trauma that may have compromised hearing or the vestibular system, but was not immediately or directly fatal."

Balcomb and Claridge deduced from these reports that, as they wrote later, "beaked whales may have a particular sensitivity to sonar acoustic stimuli at levels well below" what was previously considered "safe for cetaceans." They proposed anatomical reasons that the beaked whales suffered hemorrhages but the dolphins did not, although they pointed out that nonetheless, a spotted dolphin had fled from the sonar, too, and died.

The US Navy would eventually provide further helpful details about the training mission, which enabled scientists to reconstruct the event and determine how the sonar likely affected the whales and dolphins. The exercise was a war game to prepare ships for deployment to the Persian Gulf. They were to search for two "enemy" submarines hiding in Grand Bahama Canyon, which resembled the Strait of Gibraltar and the Strait of Hormuz between the Persian Gulf and the Gulf of Oman. Two submarines searched with passive sonar, listening for sounds emitted by the enemy subs. However, passive sonar works only when the target is moving. It was more likely that the enemy subs would be hiding, so the navy commander of the exercise ordered the surface vessels to deploy their active sonar from transmitters mounted on their hulls as they sailed down the middle of the channel. Every twenty-four seconds, a sonar transmitter would emit a "ping" that unleashed a pressure wave of 230 to 240 decibels of sound underwater.

Understanding how noise spreads in the ocean is complex, but, basically, sound travels 4.3 times faster in water than it does in air. In the waters north of Abaco Island, the warships' pulsing waves of noise would have rushed through the channel at a mile per second. Unfortunately for the cetaceans, that day, for unknown reasons, the surface waters were warmer than normal, causing the noise to travel even faster (since sound travels faster in warm waters than it does in those that are colder). Soon the upper waters in the canyon were reverberating with ear-splitting noise. For the whales and dolphins in the canyon, the pulses must have built up to the kind of ear pain many people suffer from when diving or descending too quickly in an airplane. The mammals would have been as blinded by the sound as we are by glaring light.

The cetaceans would have spent the night diving a mile or more below the waves, hunting for squid, while staying in the depths for an hour or more at a time. (A Cuvier's beaked whale holds the record for the longest and deepest recorded cetacean dive: two hours and seventeen minutes, and a depth of 9,874 feet, or 2,992 meters.) On the morning of March 15, the sonar sounds disrupted their hunts, likely causing many to attempt to flee by rushing too rapidly to the surface. Those too close to the sonar may have died from severe cranial injuries, their bodies dropping to the ocean floor. Those that managed to fight their way to the surface suffered pounding ears and cranial hemorrhages. Some may have even experienced "the bends," the decompression sickness that affects divers who surface too quickly; they likely became disoriented and were attacked by sharks, predators they could normally detect and avoid. There was nowhere to flee—other than to the beach.

Months later, Balcomb and Claridge had still seen only one of the fifty Cuvier's beaked whales they had been studying for the previous nine years, and none of the whales they rescued that March day. "We consider it entirely plausible that most, if not all, of the local population of this species was killed," they wrote, "or, at the very least, there has been a serious displacement of these whales." The two rescued minke whales were never seen again, either.

Admirably, the US Navy did at last acknowledge that its Bahamian exercise had caused the whales to strand. The navy and the NOAA issued a joint report in December 2001 explaining that the cetaceans' deaths were due to "some sort of acoustical or impulse trauma." The "most plausible source," the report concluded, was "tactical midrange frequency sonars aboard US Navy ships." The report recommended that scientists work to identify the mechanisms that caused the physiological effects leading the whales to strand, and asked the navy "to adopt measures in its future peacetime training, including those involving the use of tactical midrange sonars, to avoid the taking of marine mammals." In other words, the Office of Naval Research would provide grants to scientists to study why the sonar adversely affected cetaceans, particularly beaked whales.

BAIRD FOLLOWED THE ENTIRE Bahamian stranding saga closely. Like Balcomb, he was passionate about beaked whales, having studied them as a postdoc, and he worried about the effects of human noise on these deep-diving animals. The ocean once reverberated only with the sounds of fish calls, whale songs, winds, and storms, but by the beginning of the twenty-first century, anthropogenic sounds were drowning these out. Instead, the seas echoed with a constant industrial rumbling from tankers, ship engines, propellers, dredging, and drilling—not to mention sonar blasts—noises that sound scientists describe as "acoustic smog." The din pervades the deepest oceans and affects all marine creatures, from diminutive sea horses to giant blue whales. Now, though, there was an opportunity to begin studying how some sounds affected marine mammals.

Baird didn't have a clear project in mind, but just knowing that funds were available to investigate these questions was exciting. The ONR had announced that it was increasing its spending on marine noise research to about $6.5 million annually. It was particularly interested in studies that would pinpoint the level at which noises begin to degrade marine mammals' hearing and reveal how species like beaked whales would react to such sounds. Baird knew the navy conducted training exercises off the Hawaiian Islands. Perhaps there was a way to connect his love of beaked whales with the ONR's concerns.

Meanwhile, Baird was in North Carolina, doing necropsies (autopsies of nonhuman animals) and collecting biopsy samples from stranded bottlenose dolphins and other cetaceans—intensive work that built up his overtime hours. He used his generous comp time to return for a few weeks whenever possible to Hawai'i, where he continued his bottlenose dolphin project. In 1999 he'd started to compile a photo identification catalog of this species off Maui, and planned to continue adding more photos there and off Lana'i and the island of Hawai'i; he had a contract from the Southwest Fisheries Science Center, a regional branch of NOAA's Fisheries, to cover the costs of the work.

Although common bottlenose dolphins are a cosmopolitan species, found in tropical and temperate oceans worldwide, their wild populations are not as well studied as you might think. Dale Rice, a biologist, had observed these dolphins around the northwestern Hawaiian Islands in the late 1950s. He'd published his results in 1960 in the *Journal of Mammalogy*, and asked a question that had still not been answered when Baird began his surveys: "Are the [bottlenose dolphin] populations local and isolated, or migratory and intermingling?" In other words, are the bottlenose dolphins around the Hawaiian Islands residents, spending their lives in the coastal waters of particular islands, or did they travel far afield to mingle with other oceanic populations? Baird hoped to answer this question; his data would help government agencies better protect and manage the species.

On an early April 2002 morning, he departed Hawai'i's Honokohau (Kona) Harbor to locate dolphins. But minutes after leaving and while only two kilometers from shore, he saw a single whale surface not far from his boat. "Amazingly," Baird wrote later about this encounter, "she approached the boat, and we were able to get photos." From her log-like shape and beaky snout (or rostrum), he could see that she was a beaked whale, but he was not certain of her species. To find out, Baird fired a biopsy dart from his crossbow at the whale and collected a small skin sample. A subsequent genetic analysis of this tissue confirmed that she was a Blainville's beaked whale. After studying the photos, Baird realized a large shark (likely a white shark or tiger shark) had once taken a bite from her dorsal area, and that she'd also suffered the bites of many small cookie-cutter sharks. He and his team would use these prominent white scars to identify her many more times in the coming years.

"We got photo IDs and a biopsy sample," Baird recalled. "I think that was the first biopsy collected of this species anywhere. It was a major accomplishment and showed how even a single encounter can begin to change everything you know about a species. It helped counter the widely held perception that beaked whales were difficult to study. We gathered as much information as we could, even though we didn't have a grant to study this species. That's always been my approach, and it paid off. Those photos and biopsy sample really launched our Hawaiian beaked whale project."

Although Baird had spotted only one Blainville's beaked whale, her presence suggested that there must be more. How large was the population? Were they residents of the Hawaiian Islands or just visiting? If they were residents, they must be living in a deep ocean canyon, as did the beaked whales in the Bahamas. The US Navy also carried out sonar exercises and military war games in Hawai'i. Were these whales at risk of stranding because of the navy? And if they hadn't beached themselves during previous naval exercises, why not?

Here was a golden research opportunity—particularly because scientists would now have a population to compare with those in the Bahamas—and Baird seized it. Wasting no time, he applied for and received a grant from the Wild Whale Research Foundation, a nonprofit organization based in Hawai'i. Dan McSweeney, a captain of a whale-watching boat and a citizen-scientist, started the foundation in 1990; he'd been photographing beaked whales in the islands' waters since the mid-1980s and generously gave Baird these images. Robin planned to use the grant to assess the beaked whales' population numbers and to collect dive data on them. He would start this ten-day project in late September 2002.

When his contract with the NMFS in North Carolina ended, Baird moved to Olympia, Washington, and joined the Cascadia Research Collective, a nonprofit that provided a home for independent researchers studying marine mammals and seabirds from the Arctic to Central America. Baird offered to bring his own research dollars to the group in exchange for an office and affiliation, which gave him infrastructure, colleagues, and collaborators—and a visa. (He is now a US citizen.) From here he could easily travel to Canada to continue his killer whale studies and to Hawai'i for his research on whales and dolphins.

THROUGH THIS ONE SERENDIPITOUS encounter, Baird was on his way to becoming the leading expert on Hawai'i's beaked whales. Baird knew that finding more would be mostly a matter of luck—but luck, as he also knew, came through hard, persistent work. Like every other animal, beaked whales had regular habits; perhaps it wasn't unusual to spot them surfacing in the early morning hours outside Kona Harbor. From now on, every time he left this harbor, Baird would be on the alert for beaked whales.

Baird's hunch paid off. On September 24, 2002, again off Kona, his team encountered a group of nine: one adult male, four adult females, and four juveniles. Marine biologist Daniel Webster was with him. Webster had worked with Baird previously on a project tagging humpback whales, spotted dolphins, and other species off Maui, and on Baird's bottlenose study along the East Coast. "I don't understand the animals' behavior the way Robin does," Webster told me. "At first, I was driving the boat for him, and he was making the shots [to tag or collect biopsy samples]. But the driver is really the key to getting a good shot, and at some point, we realized that he should be driving and I should be shooting." Baird's understanding of how different species respond to the sounds and presence of a motorboat enabled him to get the boat—and Webster—in the right position to take a shot. And Webster was an excellent marksman.

"I used to shoot carp with a bow," Webster explained. "It's not something I'm proud of, but I could have done worse things." He had grown up in Colorado, where his father was an expert fly-fisher and outdoorsman. Father and son went hunting, too, and Daniel had come to love the out-of-doors. He'd attended the University of Oregon for a bachelor of science degree and had also taken courses at the Oregon Institute of Marine Biology, imagining a career as an environmentalist. The lure of surfing drew him to Hawai'i, and he'd heard through friends that Baird often used volunteers on his whale projects. They'd discovered that they were both excellent birders, able to detect from a pitching boat the fine, distinguishing wing stripes or wedge-shaped tail of a bird in the distance. And Webster could shoot. "Robin saw my potential," Webster said, "and so we teamed up."

He was with Baird that morning when the pod of nine Blainville's beaked whales came into view. The animals had likely been hunting squid and fish, and had returned to the surface to rest. They lay log-like on the water. Adult Blainville's beaked whales have grayish-brown skin typically dotted with white circles: the scars from cookie-cutter shark bites. On males, the round white marks intersect the long, rake-like white scars from fights with their rivals—a combination that can make their backs look something like celestial maps. The white scarring patterns remain visible for decades (something Baird discovered via his team's photographs), making it easy to identify individual whales. While it's not difficult to recognize a beaked whale, knowing which species you're looking at takes skill. Since his encounter with the single female earlier that year, Baird had studied numerous photographs of Blainville's and Cuvier's beaked whales. And this time he did not need a biopsy sample to identify these as the Blainville's species, which have longer rostrums than Cuvier's do and more distinct, S-shaped mouth lines.

He called to Daniel to get ready to tag one of the males. Another volunteer photographed the animals while Baird positioned the boat and Webster readied his crossbow and the suction cup radio tag. His shot hit the whale just beneath the dorsal fin and the tag stuck. The whale slapped the water with his tail and dived immediately, but soon returned to the surface and resumed resting among the other whales.

Baird followed the beaked whale for a little more than two hours before the tag fell off. Elated, he wrote a report to the Hawai'i Wildlife Fund. Once again he'd achieved a first: he and his crew had attached a time-depth recorder to a Blainville's beaked whale, and so demonstrated that it was possible to collect the kind of data the NMFS and the navy wanted.

Three days later, the crew rang up another first: They tagged an adult female Cuvier's beaked whale. This time the tag remained attached for seven hours, and Baird followed her the entire time. Ultimately, during his ten-day project, Baird and crew had three more encounters with beaked whales, both Blainville's and Cuvier's. Although their other tagging attempts failed, they photographed all the whales and collected population and behavioral data, too.

Again, Baird wasted no time in applying for more funding.

He submitted a proposal to the NMFS, which was quickly approved, and began planning for another two-month field season beginning in May 2003. He was curious about these creatures that traversed the deepest parts of the sea—and he was worried about their future. The US Navy conducted war games and sonar exercises in Hawaiian waters, putting the islands' rarest and least known cetaceans at risk of serious injury and death. Baird hoped to find out why.

9

There are twenty-two known species of beaked whales, and possibly more that have yet to be identified. Ten of these species can be found in the North Pacific, three of them in the waters that surround the Hawaiian Islands.

Each beaked whale species makes its own specific echolocation clicks, which gives scientists another way to identify the animals. Researchers have recorded the clicks of what they believe to be two additional types of beaked whales in the waters Baird patrols—species that no one has photographed yet. The scientists suspect that these other two are present because acousticians have shown via sonograms (graphs that represent sound) that the clicks of beaked whales differ from those of other whales and dolphins, and that each beaked whale species also produces species-specific clicks. What's more, they've recorded beaked whale echolocation clicks in Hawaiian waters that are not those of the known resident beaked species. With luck, Baird thinks he and his crew will one day get some proof, bringing the number of species of beaked whales that call Hawai'i home to five.

Since fortuitously happening upon the pod of Blainville's near Kona Harbor in 2002, Baird has added numerous images to his catalogs of the Hawaiian Islands' Cuvier's and Blainville's beaked whales. He's collected data on 141 whales from these species, 72 of which he's seen more than once. Over the years, his team has attached satellite tracking tags and time-depth recorders to several Cuvier's and Blainville's whales, allowing him to track the animals from his Olympia, Washington office and see which islands they travel around and how they respond to navy and industrial activities. Together the images and tagging data show clearly that both species have small resident populations off the Big Island.

The resident beaked whales live side by side here (rare for such similar species) by "partitioning the water column," Baird told me one morning as we departed Kona Harbor. Compared with Blainville's, Cuvier's beaked whales tend to prefer ocean areas that are twice as deep, so he often spots them in the deep-water regions off the east side of Hawai'i and the south side of Maui, while Blainville's keep to the shallower waters off the northwestern end of Hawai'i Island and along the Kona coast. Only the week before, a colleague photographed an adult female Blainville's with a young calf in the area we were now traveling through. He sent the photo to Baird, who recognized the whale. "We'd seen him—er, her—before," he said.

"Who was she?" I asked.

"Oh, HIMd007," Baird replied, as if saying "Sue Jones." The *HI* stands for Hawai'i and *Md* the species name, *Mesoplodon densirostris*. And she was the seventh Blainville's they'd encountered, hence the 007. Over the years, Baird's crew has gathered twenty-three records of her (from their own sightings or those of citizen-scientists), a few times with calves. It was this kind of detail that allowed Robin to assert that a population of beaked whales resides in these waters permanently—and was therefore entitled to federal protection and mitigating measures during seismic surveys or naval exercises.

During my two weeks with Baird, every time we departed or reentered Kona Harbor, he or another crew member remarked that this was a good area for spotting Blainville's beaked whales—and so, of course, I scanned the sea, hoping to spot the female and her newborn. But I never did.

On my seventh day tagging along on Baird's Zodiac, we headed northwest from the harbor toward the deeper ocean, where he hoped to show me some of Hawai'i's rarer species.

The sea was calm, a few clouds scattered far on the horizon, and Baird smiled at the conditions—perfect for sighting whales and dolphins. And yet we didn't encounter any cetaceans until after three and a half hours of searching, when, a little after nine in the morning, Baird's research associate and photographer Kimberly Wood called out from the prow, "Something splashed! Eleven o'clock. Two kilometers."

Baird studied the horizon. "Spotted dolphins," he announced, and then, for my benefit: "or more correctly, pantropical spotted dolphins." I peered in the same direction and saw dolphin-shaped animals leaping and diving through the water. How did Baird know the species from this distance?

"I look at their size, shape, and behavior, and where they live. Out here," he explained, the ocean descends to about three thousand meters, and so "we might also see rough-toothed dolphins. But they tend to dive more steeply and stick their heads out of the water when they surface. These spotted ones don't do that."

Baird increased his speed to catch up to the dolphins, which unlike the Risso's dolphins I'd seen the previous week of the survey did not shy away from the sound of motors. Daniel readied his air gun and moved toward the bow.

"Kim! Let me know if you see a good target coming in!"

Baird called to Wood. "It has to be an adult—a heavily spotted one."

"Nontargets on the bow!" Wood shouted in reply. But even these young dolphins, which love to ride a boat's bow wave, dived and vanished.

"More, straight ahead!" Webster called out. "Four hundred meters. Nontargets."

I had a closer view of the dolphins now and could see the splash of silvery white spots that cover their backs and give them their name. They're elegant, two-toned animals, their skins color blocked like race cars. Black-hued capes run from their foreheads to their tails, while their beaks, faces, sides, and bellies are a silvery gray and speckled with dark spots. They were athletic animals: some in the distance made such high, soaring leaps, they looked like they were testing what life might be like in a different element. Then they, too, dived into the blue sea and were gone.

"Well," Baird sighed as he slowed the boat, "when we have this kind of behavior, I don't think we'll have much luck tagging anyone." Webster needed an animal that was traveling, surfacing, and diving methodically. These dolphins were fishing, and would continue to dive rapidly and erratically until their hunt was finished.

As their name suggests, pantropical spotted dolphins are

Pantropical Spotted Dolphin

found worldwide in tropical seas. Most live in the deep ocean, but there are two subspecies: this one in Hawai'i (which is pelagic) and another coastal type found off the west coast of Central America. The NMFS estimates that some fifty-six thousand pantropical spotted dolphins inhabit the open ocean near the Hawaiian Islands, making them "probably the most abundant dolphin" in the region, Baird told me. But even though they're abundant, they're another little-known species. At the time of my visit, Robin and his crew had succeeded in attaching satellite tags to five of these dolphins, and they have since attached four more—all collecting data that will help us better understand these animals, their travels, and their behaviors.

Baird isn't the only person keeping an eye out for Hawai'i's spotted dolphins. Fishers have also learned to watch for where the spotteds congregate, as schools of tuna sometimes follow the dolphins in hopes of dining on their scraps. Sometimes the fishers put their trolling lines among the dolphins, which can get the spotteds inadvertently hooked on or entangled in fishing gear or struck by boat propellers. "We don't know how often they die" from these accidents, Robin told me, "and we don't know if the number of deaths affects any of the populations because we don't yet have population estimates." But elsewhere, particularly in the eastern tropical Pacific, commercial fishers have killed millions of spotted dolphins that were accidentally caught in large purse seine nets. Although fishing practices are changing, reducing the number of mortalities, the region's spotted dolphin populations have yet to recover.

Baird makes a habit of speaking to the captains of any fishing boats he comes across during his surveys, asking what they're catching and what they've seen. He talks about his research, handing out laminated photos of the species he's studying and explaining which ones are most at risk of being hooked. He's well aware that many fishers dislike dolphins and false killer whales, since they'll grab hooked fish from long lines—fishers still shoot or maim dolphins in some regions of the world—but he asks the men and women he speaks with to contact him if they see the mammals he's seeking. Some fishers regularly do.

Baird serves on an NMFS team working to reduce the number of false killer whales that fishers catch accidentally, but he doubts it has made much of a difference. He hopes his research might lead to greater government protections. But he has sympathy for the fishers, too. "They are working to make a living, and I understand that," he said. "I also like to eat fish. But it can be done sustainably and does not have to impact protected species. So, I try . . ."

WE WERE NOW 20 kilometers (12 miles) off shore, traveling over calm waters that drop to 3,600 meters (1,181 feet) below. Baird sighed. "The water is so clear and beautiful," he commented. "A perfect day for seeing more whales." During my two weeks on Baird's Zodiac, we spotted eleven species of cetaceans, including a sperm whale ("You can tell by its big, bushy blow that comes out at an angle"), pygmy sperm whales, gregarious melon-headed whales, speeding rough-toothed dolphins, and ox-like pilot whales. None of these sightings ever dampened his enthusiasm for seeing the next whale.

He leaned forward in his captain's chair. "Animals! At eleven o'clock!" he shouted, and the crew snapped to attention. "Everyone on cameras." Baird picked up speed and zoomed over the sea. "Oh, these are striped dolphins," he said as we approached. "I thought they were more spotteds. Well, we don't see these very often, either. They're pelagic— deep-sea dwellers. And they are fast!"

The dolphins raced ahead of us, bright and silvery in the morning light, leaping high to soar across the water. "Fishermen call them 'streakers,'" Baird said as he chased after the mammals, which were now making high, vaulting leaps. Wood and the others focused their cameras to capture each one. These dolphins were color blocked like the spotteds, with a dark gray cape above a silver flank and belly, and bold black stripes that ran from their eyes to their flippers and tails.

"Think we've got them all!" Wood called to Baird, letting her camera rest.

"Okay," he replied. "They aren't going to let us get close.

"So, let's collect some water samples."

As cetaceans dive through the water, they leave behind circles of smooth water called footprints. Conservation geneticist Scott Baker of the University of Oregon thinks it likely that the animals slough off skin cells as they dive, and that it might be possible to use these cells to study the cetaceans' genetics. Baird found the proposition ingenious. "We're always looking for noninvasive ways to collect data," he said, so he offered to help with Baker's project. "If this works," he told me, "we might not need to get so many biopsy samples," which would be particularly useful for species, such as striped dolphins, that he's "never succeeded in getting close enough to for a sample. So, this is a great example of how a new technique may help answer a lot of questions."

The crew had a cooler packed with jars for storing water samples. Webster pulled out one and filled it from the smooth center of a print on the starboard side. He then filled another from a print on the port side, and returned the jars to the cooler. They would later transfer the samples to Baker's lab.

"Nice," Baird said, giving a satisfied smile. "That makes two rare species for this trip today already."

He'd hoped to continue on his northwest course into ever-deeper water, but when the wind picked up, he turned the boat back toward the Big Island, ready to call it a day.

But just after noon, Wood sounded the now familiar cry: "Animals! Pilot whales at twelve o'clock. One kilometer." In the distance, we could see their dark, curved dorsal fins and the spray from their breaths.

"They're probably resting," Baird observed. They weren't bothered by our boat's approach, and soon we could make out about a dozen of the dark-hued, muscular animals, all lying calmly at the surface.

We'd encountered short-finned pilot whales almost every day. With something like twenty thousand in these waters, they're the species Baird sees the most on every survey he conducts around the Big Island. Sometimes he stopped to get photos, particularly if there were mothers with calves, which had sweet, wrinkled faces and bodies (natal folds from being scrunched inside their mothers), and always elicited cries of joy from the crew.

This time we saw only adults. They had blunt, squared-off heads and slight humps in front of their sturdy, hook-shaped dorsal fins. They weren't elegant speedsters like the dolphins, but stolid, steady souls. Baird's team has identified more than 1,200 individuals, which live in some hundred pods.

"Look at these two males." Baird pointed. "They're old, very robust, and have massive necks. Fine animals. See that hole in this one's dorsal fin?" It was large and made the fin look even more like a fishhook. "That was likely caused by a gunshot; probably an angry fisherman."

Pilot whales are highly social, Baird said; young adolescent males seem to leave their families to hang out with one another and older males in groups like the one we were watching. He slowly positioned the boat close to one of the larger animals, and Webster fired a dart, retrieving a skin and tissue sample, which he quickly removed and sealed in a tube that he then placed in the cooler. The whale slapped the water with his tail and dived, but he soon resurfaced, untroubled by the momentary sting. Two-thirds of the skin sample would be sent to the Northwest Fisheries Science Center, in Seattle, for a fungi study, while one-third would be delivered to geneticists. The blubber would be given to scientists at the University of Hawai'i who are studying stress and reproductive hormones.

"We want to find out what fungal and bacterial diseases are here in the water; what these animals have been exposed to," Baird explained. "A lot of cetacean scientists are worried now because of what happened in 2015 to L95," a twenty-year-old male killer whale who died in the waters off Vancouver Island.

Scientists found the deceased whale along the coastline five weeks after scientists from the NMFS had attached a satellite tracking tag near his dorsal fin. The tag, like those Baird uses, was designed to detach and leave nothing behind.

But a necropsy found pieces of the tag's anchors in a wound on the whale's fin. The veterinarians discovered that the biologists who'd deployed the tag had failed to attach it on their first attempt; the dart had fallen into the water and was reused without being sufficiently disinfected. At the time of his death, L95 was suffering from a skin fungus, which had somehow invaded his lungs. Perhaps the contaminated dart created an opening for the fungus to move into the whale's vascular system.

"So the question now is, 'How common is this fungus?'" Baird said. "Is it found only in that population of killer whales, which are suffering from poor nutrition and live in heavily polluted waters?" The fungus has killed several harbor porpoises in Puget Sound, in western Washington State, which suggests it's prevalent in the Pacific Northwest. What about elsewhere? The biopsy samples Baird's team collected could help answer this and other questions.

For now, Baird hasn't seen any sign that the tags his team attaches to Hawai'i's cetaceans have compromised their health. "But we also make sure we put tags only on healthy animals," he emphasized.

In Baird's view, the growing awareness of the threat pollution poses to cetaceans' health presents a great opportunity for young marine biologists. "Most marine mammals around the world live in heavily polluted waters, especially those in coastal and industrialized areas," he said. "We need more researchers to study how humans' impact on the environment is affecting marine wildlife."

Like most marine biologists, Baird is concerned about persistent organic pollutants: industrial chemicals such as polychlorinated biphenyls (PCBs), pesticides, and flame retardants that resist breaking down and make their way into the ocean from runoff, storm drains, and even airborne dust. Although PCBs were banned in the United States and much of the world in 1979, they can take a century to degrade. In the meantime, the chemicals end up in the seas, where scientists know they're accumulating in the tissues of dolphins and whales, severely damaging the animals' reproductive organs and immune systems. In Hawai'i, cetaceans such as spinner dolphins, which feed on deepwater fish and small squid, are less at risk than those that feed on larger game fish, including killer whales and false killer whales. In 2018 *Science* published an article predicting that half the world's killer whale populations are doomed to extinction due to toxic pollutants in the seas.

Environmentalists, marine veterinarians, toxicologists— are all needed to help clean up our seas, as well as nonscientists who can communicate to the public what individuals can do to reduce pollution, such as buying organic food whenever possible, as well as furniture made without flame retardants. The problem can seem daunting, and everyone, not just marine biologists, can help make the seas safe again for dolphins and whales.

SINCE THE PILOT WHALES we were trailing were large, healthy, and untroubled by our presence, Baird asked Webster to take another biopsy sample. They selected a target animal, and Baird guided the boat alongside him. Daniel fired. Like the first one he'd darted, this whale also dived after being hit—and so did another, who turned and raced toward the bow. He dropped his head beneath the Zodiac and raised his tail high, bringing it down forcefully on the water, twice—a clear sign of anger.

"Wow, a RAB!" Baird called out—a "rapid approach to boat." He wondered aloud if these whales had been harassed by tourists on Zodiacs like his; they've been known to jump into the water with whales to try to touch them. Male pilot whales have charged tour boats—and have grabbed swimmers at least twice, once taking a woman twelve meters (39 feet) below the surface before bringing her back. From 2002 to 2008, angry males often charged Baird's boat and sometimes slapped it with their tails. But then they stopped.

"We don't know why they stopped or why they're starting again," Baird told me, "but I think we'll just move on now." He backed away slowly from the whales, which were resting quietly at the surface once more.

BAIRD CONTINUES TO CONDUCT his research on cetaceans that are likely affected by sonar. The US Navy's Pacific Fleet's training and testing activities take place most often off Kaua'i. Here the navy maintains its Pacific Missile Range Facility, with its series of nearly two hundred hydrophones mounted on the seafloor to monitor its submarines and vessels. The whales and dolphins living off Kaua'i and the island of Ni'ihau are thus exposed more often to naval sonar and other naval activities than those living elsewhere in the islands, Baird said. There were resident populations of spinner, bottlenose, and rough-toothed dolphins here, as well as short-finned pilot whales. All had likely been exposed repeatedly to naval sonar.

"Is it affecting their birthrates or survival?" Baird asked rhetorically. "We don't know. We don't know what these populations were like before the navy established its bases. We do know that off Hawai'i Island there are resident populations of ten odontocete species. But only four off Kaua'i and

Ni'ihau. So, it could be that some species don't tolerate the sonar. Others may be pretty tolerant, but at what cost? Do they live shorter lives? Are their reproductive rates lower?" These were questions he hoped his research would answer some day.

The navy conducts extensive sonar testing twice a year off the northwest coast of Kaua'i. And every other year, the fleet hosts the Rim of the Pacific exercise, where the world's largest gathering of navies meets for combat drills and mock battles. When these take place, cetaceans inevitably strand—not always in huge numbers, but Baird, NOAA researchers, and marine biologist Kristi West at Hawai'i Pacific University document each incident. Following the 2014 exercises, which blasted the region with sonar that forced even human divers out of the water, three short-finned pilot whales died. Still, according to Baird, scientists "can't definitively link" the exercises to the stranded and dead whales.

The navy funds a good percentage of Baird's work. Partly with navy monies, he's investigated the diving behaviors of beaked whales, whose extreme diving abilities put them at greatest risk when sonar is deployed. Baird also watches closely for strandings. "But nothing like the Bahamas has happened here. Yet," he said.

Baird reports his findings to the navy, and urges cautious and careful management of sonar, particularly in the midfrequency range (MFA). The navy is mandated by federal law to minimize its impact on cetaceans, but Baird thinks this "mitigation" is largely ineffective. "They post a watch to look for marine mammals within a certain range," he told me, "and if they sight something, they turn off the MFA sonar." But most cetaceans react to sonar long before a human observer would see them—assuming the human notices them at all. Baird believes that implementing sonar exclusion zones would be much more effective. And it would be possible, too, since his research has identified the homes of Hawai'i's various cetaceans.

The National Resources Defense Council and other environmental groups regularly use Baird's data to challenge the navy—as they did successfully in 2015, when the navy's plans to dramatically expand its war exercises off Hawai'i and Southern California failed to include any exclusion zones. According to the settlement, the navy must restrict its use of sonar and explosives around Hawai'i—which sounds good on paper. But Baird doubts the restrictions will provide any real protection for the resident dolphins and whales, and calls the measure "a small Band-Aid."

Although much of his funding comes from the navy, he

doesn't hesitate to help environmental groups in their legal battles. "We aren't going to self-censor or change our interpretation of the data," he insisted. "If an environmental organization thinks our work is relevant to a case they're working on, I'll write it up. One reason I do the science is to help managers make good decisions. To me, that's worthwhile and satisfying. If my research is ignored, as it sometimes is with the navy, then it's frustrating. But I'm not going to stop because of concerns over losing money."

WE NEVER DID SEE beaked whales or false killer whales, the cetaceans Baird calls his "favorites" and that were the primary target of this survey and the species he most wanted to show me. He'd had a soft spot for them ever since he first came upon one on the shores of Denman Island, just off Vancouver Island, where it had stranded in 1987. That was the first time anyone had ever seen a false killer whale in Canada—and was Baird's first encounter with such a rare species.

Highly social animals, they are often curious about people. False killer whales are so at ease around humans that they sometimes offer them the fish they'd killed. "I've never had that experience," Baird said, "but I've seen them pass a fish back and forth among all the members of their group before giving it back to the one who caught it. Then they all get a share." Baird smiled at the thought of this very human-like behavior, which is one way "they build social bonds—just like when you invite friends to dinner."

Although Baird rarely encountered this species in Hawai'i, he and his crew had gathered as much data as possible whenever they did. As a result, false killer whales are now one of the best-known cetacean species in the islands; Baird's data also had helped place them on the federal endangered species list. "It's the population that's most at risk here," he said, from pollutants, overfishing, and being caught by fishers.

We were motoring parallel to the Big Island now, which rose like a giant green fin from the sea, and met up with a group of rowdy rough-toothed dolphins that were hunting squid. Webster used a net to snag a partially damaged squid that a Bulwer's petrel, a small seabird, had scavenged from the dolphins. Daniel placed the squid in a collecting jar and stored this in the cooler. Curious about the food so many of the cetacean species dine on here, Baird had asked his crew in 2006 to begin collecting squid like this one. Now they had about 110 specimens. "Virtually nothing is known about them," Baird said. "It's another rich diversity of species that needs documenting."

We continued our search, but across a sea that looked utterly calm. No fins, spouts, or splashes—at least none that I could see. Just then Cornforth shouted, *"Feresa!* At two o'clock," and the crew leaped up, cameras snapping. Baird slipped the boat into neutral as we drifted toward the animals: a small pod of pygmy killer whales that were resting at the surface but began what's called spy hopping: that is, standing upright in the water, with their dark, rounded heads poking just above the surface. "They are so hard to see when they do this," Baird said, "but I think I recognize a couple of them from the white scars on their faces. They like to look at people in boats but are also easily spooked."

He wanted to get a biopsy, but worried that "they're smart enough to make a connection between our boat and the dart. Then they might avoid us in the future." Ultimately, we left them in peace.

Looking out over the blue waters that surround Hawai'i, you wouldn't suspect that so many cetaceans live here, hidden in its depths like the most perfectly camouflaged birds in a forest. Baird and his crew worked long, sometimes tedious hours each day to find the animals he showed me, often traveling atop a sea as bright as metal as the hot sun beat down. Even when we did find whales to watch, we were limited in what we could see and know about them. With a flick of their tails, they slipped away, leaving us—and our unanswered questions—behind.

Baird and his crew rarely showed frustration about their work or the animals they sought. They were here because of their love for whales and dolphins, and for the sea, and their hope to pass on that love—and the concern that went with it—to others.

It was after two o'clock by the time Baird turned back to Kona Harbor. We'd traveled a little more than a hundred miles this day. He stood at the Zodiac's helm, where Webster joined him. Side by side, they scanned the sea. Baird opened a package of saltines for a late lunch and offered the crackers to Webster.

"Livin' the dream, right?" Webster asked with a wry smile as he bit into a dry saltine.

Baird guffawed. "Oh, yes," he said. "We're livin' the dream."

Epilogue

F or readers who hope one day to fulfill their own dream of becoming a marine biologist, Robin Baird offers this advice: "Never admit that you love whales," he said, or any other "charismatic" creature you may be studying—even though of course you do. As a young scientist, he'd discovered that line was sure to sink any conversation with more experienced researchers.

"When you're at meetings," he explained, "where there are other grad students working on insects, mice, viruses," and you're gushing about your awesome research interest, people aren't apt to take you seriously. But if you said, "I'm working on optimal foraging group size," other scientists would listen to you and offer advice.

Whales in particular have a reputation for attracting enthusiasts with unconventional New Age beliefs, an unfortunate association that developed after neurophysiologist John Lilly reported having conversations with bottlenose dolphins in the 1960s. While Lilly's books have inspired many young people to become marine biologists, quoting him or others who regard cetaceans as ancient, sophisticated beings with unique knowledge to communicate to humans is not going to win you much respect as a scientist.

Just as it's not wise to lead with your love of cetaceans, it's also not a good idea to set your heart on any one species. "While a lot of kids think about studying dolphins or killer whales," Baird told me, "they'll find that there are many, many species just as fascinating. The world is a really interesting place, and there are lots of interesting questions to be asked about fish, squid, and jellies"—as well as aquatic plants and microscopic organisms. Being open to studying lesser known species will broaden your career opportunities.

Baird urges hopeful marine biologists to read the existing scientific literature—published articles and books—to figure out which questions have already been asked and answered; doing so will also help them learn how to ask questions. When Baird was an undergraduate, he and his girlfriend, Pamela Stacey (who was also studying to become a marine biologist), spent their evenings together reading the latest papers on marine mammals. Killer whale researcher Dr. Andrew Foote at Switzerland's University of Bern echoes Baird's advice to read voraciously and widely, nudging the students he meets at conferences to not "limit your reading and studies to just marine mammals." If you're knowledgeable about findings in other fields, you'll be able to put your work into a "broader biological context," he explained, making it more meaningful.

You don't have to do this all on your own. Look for mentors who can guide you in new directions and help you think about bigger questions. Richard Connor, a cetacean biologist at the University of Massachusetts and codirector of The Dolphin Alliance Project, Inc., a nonprofit organization dedicated to solving the mystery of dolphin intelligence, studied for his PhD under chimpanzee expert Richard Wrangham. Not only was Connor far from the sea—at the University of Michigan—he was also the only student in his classes studying marine mammals; everyone else was focused on primates. However, Connor was interested in studying dolphins' social intelligence: a skill that requires being able to cooperate with others who are not your kin and is believed to have driven the evolution of intelligence in many species. When applying to PhD programs, he was astute enough to determine that Wrangham, an expert on social cognition, was the right mentor for him.

As an undergraduate, it's best to major in biology or zoology (not marine biology); you can specialize later in grad school. It's also wise to take the recommended math and statistics courses; science is about measuring and quantifying the world, and you will need these skills. You don't have to have the strongest background in these subjects—Baird didn't—but if you hope to successfully analyze research data, you'll need a solid foundation in at least the basics.

Academics are important, but it's also essential to have a diverse set of extracurricular skills. "Marine biology is a competitive field," Baird stressed in our conversations, "and people need to stand out or excel in some way." You might, for instance, master a practical skill that will prove useful on field projects, such as training as an outboard motor mechanic. To develop your observational skills, you might become a birdwatcher, perhaps by joining a local chapter of the National Audubon Society, which sponsors free birding walks with experts. And Baird is always looking for interns who can program the data collection tags he deploys or who can write clearly about science.

You should also gain a feeling for what it's like to be a marine biologist day in and day out by applying for internships, volunteering—if you're fortunate enough to live on one of the coasts, offer to help out at a local maritime museum or public aquarium—or joining an organization such as the Society for Marine Mammalogy, the American Academy of Underwater Sciences, the National Association of Marine Laboratories, the Oceanography Society, or the Marine Conservation Institute, many of which offer workshops for students. If your heart is set on becoming a cetacean biologist, try volunteering with a stranding network, or get a job on a whale-watching boat, even if it's just as a deckhand. "Many of the people working at Cascadia started as volunteers or interns," Baird told me. "And that reflects the way that marine biology is heading these days. People earn a degree, but then they need to get practical experience, and that typically comes by volunteering or through an internship, positions that are often unpaid." This can present a financial hardship for many, but Baird has found that students who manage to juggle volunteer work with earning an income often fare better in the long run. "I want volunteers and interns who have initiative," he said, "and who are self-motivated. That is something that's not taught in schools. It's taught in life."

Is it possible to change careers or switch specialties later in life? Tiu Similä, from Finland did. She was finishing her graduate studies at Helsinki University, studying the phytoplankton (microscopic algae) of Finnish lakes, when she lost her heart to Norway's killer whales.

Phytoplankton use sunlight to convert carbon dioxide into sugars, giving off oxygen in the process. They are an essential part of the food web in bodies of water, from creeks to oceans, getting fed on by zooplankton (tiny animals), shellfish, and fish, which are in turn eaten by larger animals, including baleen whales such as humpbacks and grays. Similä's interest in plankton led her to read more about whales in general. To her surprise, "there was very little written about whales in Finnish," she recalled. Shockingly, "most of the species did not even have names" in that language. She and her academic advisor decided to write a book together to fill in this gap.

Similä began collecting information about and photographs of cetaceans from across Scandinavia, a search that led her to a group of Danish and Swedish biologists and artists who had just launched the first field study of killer whales in the Arctic waters around Norway's Lofoten Islands. When she asked for photos of the orcas, the group told her to "come and take them" herself. So she did. After a heart-stopping encounter with a male killer whale, she dropped her plankton project, transferred to the University of Tromsø in Norway, and began studying orcas.

No one discouraged Similä, and perhaps more important, a leading Finnish conservation biologist, Ilkka Hanski, actually encouraged her. Similä has since become the world's leading authority on Norway's killer whales.

Certainly, Similä's career path was unorthodox. And while her passion helped carry her through some hard times, such as when funds were low—as of 2017, the median pay for a marine biologist was $62,290 annually—Similä warned that passion alone was not sufficient. "Students are often surprised at how much hard and tedious work is required" to succeed in the profession, she told me. "If you are not willing to work systematically and on tiresome data analysis, such as photo identification studies, you should not start studying animals. You will need buckets of patience and a huge amount of motivation to find the answers to your questions."

Marine biologists don't simply study one species; they must also determine the role each organism plays in the marine ecosystem. Scientists are still investigating what researchers who used dredges and trawling devices in the nineteenth century also sought to understand: which species live in the various layers of the ocean, and how they interact and contribute to the health of the sea. Today's marine biologists strive to maintain the diversity of organisms that dwell throughout the seas, as marine animals contend with the ever-increasing negative effects of human activities, such as pollution, entanglements, overfishing, and noise, as well as the growing threat of climate change and ocean acidification. There are sure to be jobs for marine biologists interested in addressing these concerns in the years to come, although the US Bureau of Labor Statistics does caution that "because most funding comes from governmental agencies, demand for zoologists and wildlife biologists will be limited by budgetary constraints."

Still, there are reasons for optimism. Technological advances have produced exciting inventions such as manned submersibles (like the newly reconfigured Alvin, which is designed to carry scientists to twenty thousand feet [6,096 meters] below) and remotely operated underwater vehicles (ROVs) that allow scientists to explore the deep-sea world much as William Beebe envisioned a century ago. Outfitted with high-output lights, broadcast-quality video cameras, and special collecting equipment, ROVs can be deployed from ships at sea. Researchers can watch in real time on onboard monitors as their ROV descends through the marine snow: the constant shower of organic detritus that falls from the ocean's surface into the midnight dark of the aphotic zone, some 660 to 3,280 feet (200 to 1,000 meters) below. From there, it is utterly dark to the bottommost part of the sea, the

Mariana Trench, some 36,070 feet (10,994 meters) below the surface. Yet life persists, without sunlight or oxygen.

The creatures in these depths thrive around hydrothermal vents: geysers on the seafloor that expel superheated, mineral-rich water. These vents often form tall, craggy structures called black smokers, which support colonies of chemosynthetic bacteria and archaea (single-celled microorganisms). Instead of using sunlight for energy, these microbes rely on chemicals such as hydrogen sulfide, produced by the smokers. The black smokers are typically teeming with life, encrusted with mats of bacteria and complex communities of bacteria-feeding giant tube worms, spider crabs, giant clams, shrimp, and limpets, which in turn support squids, octopuses, hatchetfish, and other organisms.

The discovery that life can exist at such great depths, supported by chemicals rather than sunlight and in anaerobic (oxygen-free) conditions, has opened new avenues of research for marine biologists, who are now joining the search for life on other planets and beyond our solar system, a field known as exobiology. Marine microbiologists, in particular, will be needed to help survey the oceans on several of the moons of Jupiter and Saturn, including Europa and Enceladus, where active hydrothermal vents are thought to exist.

In her 1951 classic *The Sea Around Us*, Rachel Carson

called the ocean "that great mother of life." She may be more correct than she could ever have known. In 1990 German chemist Günter Wächtershäuser proposed that life on Earth originated at hydrothermal vents on the seafloor, an idea that has energized the marine microbiological community. If Wächtershäuser's hypothesis proves correct, then scientists believe it is likely that life will be found elsewhere in our universe—not only on the moons of other planets in our solar system, but also in the as yet undiscovered seas of planetary bodies coursing through space. Marine biologists are ready to start looking.

SOURCES

INTERVIEWS

Robin Baird kindly made time for interviews during his June 2017 Hawaiian cetacean survey; I interviewed him or recorded (in handwritten notes) comments he made while on board his Zodiac and at his rental home in Kona, Hawai'i. I also interviewed him by telephone several times both before and after the survey, and also sent him questions via email, which he always graciously answered.

On board the Zodiac, I used Rite in the Rain notebooks to jot down comments the crew members made about the survey, their work, and cetacean sightings, and also interviewed them about their backgrounds in marine biology/cetacean watching and how they'd joined Baird's crew.

In addition, I interviewed by telephone these colleagues of Baird's: conservation geneticist and cetacean expert Dr. Scott Baker at the Marine Mammal Institute, Oregon State University; marine biologist Dr. Dave Duffus at University of Victoria, British Columbia, Canada; Dr. Larry Dill, marine biologist and ecologist at Simon Fraser University, Vancouver, British Columbia; and cetacean expert and marine biologist Dr. Hal Whitehead at Dalhousie University, Halifax, Nova Scotia, Canada. For the last chapter, I used material from a previous interview with Dr. Tiu Similä in Norway for a *National Geographic* article about the orcas of Norway ("How Orcas Work Together to Whip

Up a Meal," *National Geographic*, July 2015); and I also used material from my interviews with Dr. Richard Connor at his dolphin study site, Shark Bay, Australia, for my book *Animal Wise: How We Know Animals Think and Feel*. I also interviewed by telephone Dr. John Delaney at the University of Washington, Seattle, about his research exploring deep-sea volcanoes and deploying networked observatories on the ocean floor.

I've checked details with Baird and his team, but any errors are my own.

CHAPTER 3

43 *"peer out and actually see"*: Beebe, *Half Mile Down*, 134–35.

43 *"colors and absence of colors . . ."*: William Beebe, *Adventuring with Beebe: Selections from the Writings of William Beebe* (New York: Viking Press, 1955), 84.

43 *"below the level of humanly visual light"* . . . *deep-sea snails* . . . and *"all brilliantly lighted"*: Beebe, *Half Mile Down*, 164–65.

44 *"We need a whole new vocabulary"*: William Beebe, "A Round Trip to Davy Jones's Locker, *National Geographic*, June 1931, 665.

46 *"I stood upside down"*: Capt. Jacques-Yves Cousteau with Frédéric Dumas, *The Silent World* (Washington, DC: National Geographic Society, 2004), 4.

46 *"Delivered from gravity"*: Ibid., 4.

46 *"I reached the bottom"*: Ibid., 3.

47 *"from this day forward . . . fish scales know"*: Ibid.

51 *"We all owe a debt"* . . . : Susan Farady, quoted in "Ocean Careers: Jacques Cousteau: Ocean Exploration Pioneer," National Oceanic and Atmospheric Administration online, last modified July 31, 2017, https://sanctuaries.noaa.gov/news/features/jacques_cousteau.html.Bibliography.

CHAPTER 4

54 *"the most likely reason"*: Peter Jones, Alison Cathcart, and Douglas C. Spiers, "Early Evidence of the Impact of Preindustrial Fishing on Fish Stocks from the Mid-west and Southeast Coastal Fisheries of Scotland in the 19th Century," ICES *Journal of Marine Science* 73, no. 5 (May 1, 2016): 1404–14.

56 *"I believe . . . that the cod fishery"*: Thomas Henry Huxley, Inaugural Address, Fisheries Exhibition, London, 1883, Clark University online, accessed November 28, 2018. https://mathcs .clarku.edu/huxley/SM5/fish.html

57 *"taking too much fish"*: Edward Ricketts to Joseph Campbell, 1946, in Stephen R. Palumbi and Carolyn Sotka, *The Death and Life of Monterey Bay: A Story of Revival* (Washington, DC: Island Press, 2011), https://epdf.tips/the-death-and-life-of-monterey-bay-a-story-of-rev.

58 *"refused to listen"*: Edward F. Ricketts, "Scientists Report on Sardine Supply": Investigator Blames Industry, Nature for Shortage," *Monterey Peninsula Herald* online, April 2, 1948, www .naturespeace.org/ed_ricketts1948sardine.htm.

58 *"This year, with the sardine"*: Edward F. Ricketts, "Science Studies the Sardine: Mysterious Disappearance Focuses Attention on Woeful Lack of Information Regarding Billion Dollar Fish," *Monterey Peninsula Herald* online, March 7, 1947, www .datadeluge.com/2009/06/science-studies-sardine-mysterious_27 .html.

59 *"extends beyond the limits"*: Daniel Hawthorne and Frances Minot, *The Inexhaustible Sea* (New York: Dodd, Mead, 1954), 258.

59 *"on the belief that"*: Michael L. Weber, *From Abundance to Scarcity: A History of U.S. Marine Fisheries Policy* (Washington, DC: Island Press, 2001), xxii.

61 *"[M]an . . . cannot control"*: Rachel Carson, *The Sea Around Us* (New York: Oxford University Press, NY, 1961), 15.

62 *"[T]he belief that"*: Ibid., xi.

64 *"We saw daily great"*: William Bradford and Edward Winslow, in *The Journal of the Pilgrims at Plymouth, in New England, in 1620*, quoted by New Bedford Whaling Museum online, last modified August 3, 2016, www.whalingmuseum.org/learn/research-topics/overview-of-north-american-whaling/american-whaling.

67 *"The sperm whales"* . . . *"limited than theirs"*: John C. Lilly, *The Mind of the Dolphin: A Nonhuman Intelligence* (Garden City, NY: Doubleday, 1967), 55.

69 *"[T]hat was the moment"*: Rex Weyler quoted in *How to Change the World*, a 2015 film written and directed by Jerry Rothwell.

69 *"saving the whales"*: Charlotte Epstein quoted in Karl Mathiesen, "How to Change the World: Greenpeace and the Power of the Mindbomb," *Guardian* (US edition) online, last modified June 11, 2015, www.theguardian.com/environment/2015/jun/11/how-to-change-the-world-greenpeace-power-mindbomb.

CHAPTER 5

73 *"Killer whales ceased"*: David Neiwart, *Of Orcas and Men: What Killer Whales Can Teach Us* (New York: Overlook Press, 2015), 117.

74 *"the same size"*: Erich Hoyt, *Orca: The Whale Called Killer* (Richmond Hill, Ont.: Firefly Books, 1990).

75 *"killer whales"* . . . *"killer apes"*: Paul Spong, quoted by Mark Leiren-Young, in Michael Ruffolo, " 'The Killer Whale Who Changed the World': Q&A with Mark Leiren-Young, Whose Forthcoming Book Looks at Moby Doll, the First Orca Captured and Put on Display," *Tyee*, September 7, 2016, https://thetyee.ca/Culture/2016/09/07/Killer-Whale-Who-Changed-World.

78   *"ratty little groups"*: Mike Bigg, quoted in John K. B. Ford and
      Graeme M. Ellis, *Transients Mammal-Hunting Killer Whales*
      (Seattle: University of Washington Press, 1999), 7.

80   *"tend to be . . . easy to lose"*: Ford, John K.B. and Graeme M. Ellis,
      in *Transients*, 10.

88   *" chases" . . . "clearing the water"*: Baird, *Killer Whales of the World*,
      17.

89   *"the two adults"*: Ibid., 16.

90   *"transients are probably"*: Michael A. Bigg et al., *Killer Whales: A
      Study of Their Identification, Genealogy & Natural History in British
      Columbia and Washington State* (Nanaimo, BC, Phantom Press,
      1987), 11; Virginia Morell, "Killer Whales Earn Their Name,"
      Science 331, no. 6015 (January 21, 2011): 274–76, http://science
      .sciencemag.org/content/331/6015/274.

90   *"should be considered"*: Robin Baird, "Foraging Behavior and
      Ecology of Transient Killer Whales (*Orcinus orca*)" (PhD thesis,
      Simon Fraser University, 1994), 145, www.cascadiaresearch.org/
      staff/robin-baird/foraging-behavior-and-ecology-transient-
      killer-whales-orcinus-orca.

CHAPTER 8

123   *"What in the world?"*: Jason Horwitz, *War of the Whales* (New
      York: Simon & Schuster, 2014), 7.

129   *"the notion that bats might"*: "Donald R. Griffin," *Biographical
      Memoirs*, vol. 86 (Washington, DC: National Academies Press,
      2005), 195, http://doi:10.17226/11429.

135   *"upgraded the sonar threat"*: Horwitz, *War of the Whales*, 255.

135   *"injuries consistent with"*: "Joint Interim Report: Bahamas Marine
      Mammal Stranding Event of 15–16 March 2000" (December
      2001, Washington D.C.: U.S. Department of Commerce and
      Department of the Navy), 22, https://repository.library.noaa

.gov/view/noaa/16198/noaa_16198_DS1; Kenneth C. Balcomb III and Diane E. Claridge, "A Mass Stranding of Whales Caused by Naval Sonar in the Bahamas," *Bahamas Journal of Science*, 8 no. 2 (May 1, 2001): 4–6, www.bahamaswhales.org/Stranding_Article .pdf.

135   *"significant cranial lesions"*: T. Rowles et. al., "Mass Stranding of Multiple Cetacean Species in the Bahamas, March 15–17, 2000: Draft Report to the International Whaling Commission" (unpublished report, document SC/52/E28); Society of Marine Mammalogy online.

138   *"some sort of"* . . . *"US Navy ships"*: "Joint Interim Report: Bahamas Marine Mammal Stranding," 47.

138   *"to adopt measures . . . taking of marine mammals"*: Ibid., 48.

138   *Office of Naval Research*: Office of Naval Research online, accessed November 28, 2018, www.onr.navy.mil.

FURTHER READING

All of Robin Baird's scientific articles are available at no cost on the Cascadia Research Collective's website: www.cascadiaresearch.org/staff/robin-baird/robin-w-baird-publications.

In addition to Baird's articles, I used and/or quoted from the following sources:

CHAPTERS 1 & 2

Baird, Robin. *Killer Whales of the World: Natural History and Conservation*. St. Paul, MN: Voyageur Press, 2006.
———. *The Lives of Hawai'i's Dolphins and Whales: Natural History and Conservation*. University of Hawai'i Press, Honolulu, 2016.

CHAPTER 3

Readers can find a helpful history of marine biology at the MarineBio Conservation Society's (MBSC) website: http://marinebio.org/oceans/history-of-marine-biology. The MBSC site also has useful information about education requirements, careers, and the many conservation issues challenging the oceans and marine biologists today (http://marinebio.org). The National Oceanic and Atmospheric Administration (NOAA) maintains a website about ocean exploration in the United States, beginning in 1807 when Thomas Jefferson authorized the Survey of the Coast: https://oceanexplorer.noaa.gov/history/history.html.

Beebe, William. *Half Mile Down*. New York: Harcourt, Brace, 1934.

Roberts, Callum, *The Unnatural History of the Sea*. Washington, DC: Island Press, 2008.

Stott, Rebecca. *Darwin and the Barnacle: The Story of One Tiny Creature and History's Most Spectacular Scientific Breakthrough*. New York: W. W. Norton, 2004.

CHAPTER 4

Carson, Rachel, *The Sea Around Us*. New York: Oxford University Press, 1961.

Cousteau, Capt. Jacques-Yves, with Frédéric Dumas. *The Silent World*. Washington, DC: National Geographic Society, 2004.

Harwood, John. "Marine Mammals and Their Environment in the Twenty-first Century." *Journal of Mammalogy* 82, no. 3 (August 1, 2001): 630–40, https://doi.org/10.1644/1545-1542(2001)082<0630:MMATEI>2.0.CO;2.

Jackson, Jeremy B. C., Karen E. Alexander, and Enric Sala. *Shifting Baselines: The Past and the Future of Ocean Fisheries*. Washington, DC: Island Press, 2011.

Kunzig, Robert. *Mapping the Deep: The Extraordinary Story of Ocean Science*. New York: W. W. Norton, 2000.

Levinton, Jeffrey S. *Marine Biology: Function, Biodiversity, Ecology*. New York: Oxford University Press, 2001.

Mann, Janet, Richard C. Connor, Peter L. Tyack, and Hal Whitehead, eds. *Cetacean Societies: Field Studies of Dolphins and Whales*. Chicago: University of Chicago Press, 2000.

Morell, Virginia. "Can Science Keep Alaska's Pollock Fishery Healthy?" *Science* 326, no. 5958, (December 4, 2009): 1340–41, http://science.sciencemag.org/content/326/5958/1340.

Norse, Elliott A., and Larry B. Crowder, eds. *Marine Conservation*

Biology: The Science of Maintaining the Sea's Biodiversity.
Washington, DC: Island Press, 2005.

Safina, Carl. *Song for the Blue Ocean: Encounters Along the World's Coasts and Beneath the Seas.* New York: Henry Holt, 1998.

Worm, Boris. "Averting a Global Fisheries Disaster." Proceedings of the National Academy of Sciences of the United States of America 113, no. 18 (May 3, 2016): 4895–97, www.ncbi.nlm.nih .gov/pmc/articles/PMC4983826.

Worm, Boris, Edward B. Barbier, Nicola Beaumont, J. Emmett Duffy, Carl Folke, Benjamin S. Halpern, Jeremy B. C. Jackson et al. "Impacts of Biodiversity Loss on Ocean Ecosystem Services." *Science* 314, no. 5800 (November 3, 2006): 787–90.

CHAPTER 5

Beebe, William. *Half Mile Down.* New York, Harcourt, Brace, 1934.

Bigg, Michael A., Graeme Ellis, John K. B. Ford, and Kenneth C. Balcomb. *Killer Whales: A Study of Their Identification, Genealogy & Natural History in British Columbia and Washington State.* Nanaimo, BC: Phantom Press, 1987.

Burnett, D. Graham. *The Sounding of the Whale: Science & Cetaceans in the Twentieth Century.* Chicago: University of Chicago Press, 2012.

Colby, Jason M., *Orca: How We Came to Know and Love the Ocean's Greatest Predator.* New York: Oxford University Press, 2018.

Connor, Richard, *Dolphin Politics in Shark Bay: A Journey of Discovery.* Australia: Dolphin Alliance Project, 2018.

Ellis, Richard. *Men & Whales.* New York: Alfred A. Knopf, 1991.

Ford, John K. B., and Graeme M. Ellis. *Transients: Mammal-Hunting Killer Whales.* Seattle: University of Washington Press, 1999.

Hoyt, Erich. *Creatures of the Deep: In Search of the Sea's Monsters and the World They Live In.* Richmond Hill, Ont.: Firefly Books, 2014.

————. *Orca: The Whale Called Killer*. Richmond Hill, Ont.: Firefly Books, 1990.

Neiwert, David. *Of Orcas and Men: What Killer Whales Can Teach Us*. New York: Overlook Press, 2015.

CHAPTER 6

Whitehead, Hal, and Luke Rendell. *The Cultural Lives of Whales and Dolphins*. Chicago: University of Chicago Press, 2015.

CHAPTER 7

Online Resources

Keiko: The Untold Story of the Star of Free Willy, documentary trailer, produced/directed by Theresa Demarest (2011, Joshua Records), www.keikotheuntoldstory.com/.

"Marine Mammals: Keiko," Jean-Michel Cousteau's Ocean Futures Society online, accessed _November 28, 2018, www .oceanfutures.org/action/marine-mammals/keiko.

Pacific Whale Foundation online accessed November 28, 2018, www .pacificwhale.org/cruises/maui-whalewatch.

Hawaiian Islands Humpback Whale National Marine Sanctuary online, accessed November 28, 2019, https://hawaiihumpbackwhale .noaa.gov.

CHAPTER 8

Horwitz, Joshua. *War of the Whales: A True Story*. New York: Simon & Schuster, 2014.

Twiss, John R., Jr., and Randall R. Reeves, eds. *Conservation and Management of Marine Mammals*. Washington, DC: Smithsonian Institution Press, 1999.

EPILOGUE

Brazil, Rachel. "Life's Origins: By Land or Sea? Debate Gets Hot." *Chemistry World*, May 15, 2017, www.scientificamerican.com/article/lifes-origins-by-land-or-sea-debate-gets-hot.

Stenersen, John, and Tiu Similä. *Norwegian Killer Whales*. Oslo, Nor: Tringa Forlag, 2004.

Online Resources

Suzanne Jacobs, "How Do You Study an Underwater Volcano? Build an Underwater Laboratory," University of Washington School of Oceanography online, last modified August 18, 2015, www.ocean.washington.edu/story/How_do_you.

Hannah Hickey, "Underwater Volcano: Seafloor Sensors Record Possible Eruption of Underwater Volcano," University of Washington School of Oceanography online, last modified April 30, 2015, www.ocean.washington.edu/story/Underwater_Volcano.

Ocean Observatories Initiative online, accessed _November 24, 2018, https://oceanobservatories.org.

"Discovering Hydrothermal Vents: 1979: The 'Smoking' Gun," Woods Hole Oceanographic Institution online, accessed November 24, 2018, www.whoi.edu/feature/history-hydrothermal-vents/discovery/1979-2.html.

"Are There Oceans on Other Planets? Earth Is the Only Known Planet to Have Bodies of Liquid Water on Its Surface," National Ocean Service online, last modified October 1, 2018, https://oceanservice.noaa.gov/facts/et-oceans.html.

Daniel Strain, "Icy Moons of Saturn and Jupiter May Have Conditions Needed for Life," UC Santa Cruz Newscenter, last modified December 14, 2009, https://news.ucsc.edu/2009/12/3443.html.

James Cameron's Deepsea Challenge, documentary trailer, Directors, John

Bruno, Andrew Wight, Ray Quint; Producers, James Cameron, Brett Popplewell, 2004, National Geographic Films, www.deepseachallenge.com.

Smithsonian Ocean Team, "From Submarines to Robots: Exploring the Deep Ocean," Smithsonian Institution online, last modified December 2009, https://ocean.si.edu/ecosystems/deep-sea/submarines-robots-exploring-deep-ocean.

Emily Frost, "Personal Perspectives: Keeping Exploration Alive with Manned Submersibles," Smithsonian Institution online, last modified October 2015, https://ocean.si.edu/human-connections/exploration/keeping-exploration-alive-manned-submersibles.

Online Advice for Becoming a Marine Biologist

Robin Baird, "Advice for People Interested in a Career Studying Marine Mammals." Cascadia Research Collective online, last modified, May 2018, www.cascadiaresearch.org/staff/robin-baird/advice.

"UW Announces New Marine Biology Major," University of Washington School of Oceanography online, accessed November 28, 2018, www.ocean.washington.edu/story/UW_Announces_New_Marine_Biology_Major. "How to Become a Marine Biologist: Education and Career Roadmap," Study.com, accessed November 24, 2018. https://study.com/articles/How_to_Become_a_Marine_Biologist_Education_and_Career_Roadmap.html.

"How to Become a Marine Biologist," HowtoBecome.com, accessed November 24, 2018, www.howtobecome.com/how-to-become-a-marine-biologist."5 Steps: Experience and Education Needed to Become a Marine Biologist," Ecology Project International online, accessed November 24, 2018, www.ecologyproject.org/about/blog/5-steps-experience-and-education-needed-to-become-a-marine-biologist.

"Learn How to Become a Marine Biologist—Qualification
      Requirements & Expected Salary,"
Land Your Life, last modified August 29, 2018, www.landyourlife.com
      /marine-biologist."Becoming a Marine Biologist," Stony Brook
      University online, accessed November 24, 2018, http://life.bio
      .sunysb.edu/marinebio/becoming.html.
Tania Militello, "So You Think You Want to Be a Marine Biologist?,"
      WiseOceans (blog), last modified June 25, 2015, www.wiseoceans
      .com/so-you-think-you-want-to-be-a-marine-biologist. "Marine
      Careers," Marinecareers.net, accessed November 28, 2018, www
      .marinecareers.net/marine-biology.
"Ocean Exploration Careers: Dr. Timothy Shank," Ocean Exploration
      and Research online, accessed November 18, 2018, https://
      oceanexplorer.noaa.gov/edu/oceanage/05shank/welcome.html.

Get Involved: Institutions and Organizations

American Academy of Underwater Sciences (AAUS), www.aaus.org.
International Whaling Commission, https://iwc.int/home.
Marine Conservation Institute, https://marine-conservation.org.
Monterey Bay Aquarium Research Institute (MBARI), www.mbari.org.
Marine Biological Laboratory (MBL) of Woods Hole, www.mbl.edu.
National Association of Marine Laboratories (NAML), www.naml.org.
The Oceanography Society (TOS), https://tos.org.
Oregon Institute of Marine Biology (OIMB), https://oimb.uoregon.edu.
Organization of Biological Field Stations (OBFS), www.obfs.org.
Pelagic Shark Research Foundation (PSRF), www.pelagic.org.
Scripps Institution of Oceanography, https://scripps.ucsd.edu.
Smithsonian Institution Ocean Portal, https://ocean.si.edu.
Society for Marine Mammalogy (SMM), www.marinemammalscience
      .org.
UC Santa Cruz Institute of Marine Sciences, https://ims.ucsc.edu.

ABOUT THE AUTHOR

VIRGINIA MORELL is a regular contributor to *National Geographic* magazine and a contributing correspondent to *Science*. She has also written for *Smithsonian, Discover, The New York Times Magazine, International Wildlife, Audubon, Slate,* and *Outside,* among other publications. She and her husband, writer Michael McRae, live in southern Oregon, on the edge of the Siskiyou Mountains, where they hike every day with their Scotch Collies, Buckaroo and Annie Oakley.